Events That Changed the Course of History

The Story of
APOLLO 11
AND THE MEN ON THE MOON
50 YEARS LATER

By Myra Faye Turner

EVENTS THAT CHANGED THE COURSE OF HISTORY: THE STORY OF APOLLO 11 AND THE MEN ON THE MOON 50 YEARS LATER

1405 SW 6th Avenue • Ocala, Florida 34471 • Phone 800-814-1132 • Fax 352-622-1875
Website: www.atlantic-pub.com • Email: sales@atlantic-pub.com
SAN Number: 268-1250

Library of Congress Cataloging-in-Publication Data

Names: Turner, Myra Faye, author.
Title: The story of Apollo 11 and the men on the moon 50 years later / by Myra Faye Turner.
Description: Ocala, Florida : Atlantic Publishing Group, Inc., [2018] |
Series: Events that changed the course of history | Summary: "Imagine being far enough from the earth that it looks like a tiny blue circle. In July 1969, three men aboard the Apollo spaceship got to see just that on their way to the moon. The moon landing is an unforgettable episode in American history. For centuries, going to the moon had seemed like an interesting idea, but surely impossible. But as various technologies developed at a rapid pace in the mid-20th century, the impossible became possible. You've surely heard of Armstrong's famous words, "That's one small step for man, one giant leap for mankind." But there's probably a lot that you don't know. Get ready to discover the following: - The debate behind Armstrong's famous words - The contents of the poem that Pat Collins gave her husband before he left Earth - The adrenaline rush of the three astronauts when Apollo 11 launched - How the astronauts dealt with TV cameras to provide video footage - The complex responsibilities of managing a spaceship 50 years ago Even if you've heard recordings of Neil Armstrong's voice many times, when you immerse yourself in the dramatic events of July 1969, you'll unearth the significance and fascination of this famous historical event"— Provided by publisher. | Includes bibliographical references and index |
Audience: Grade 9 to 12
Identifiers: LCCN 2017057653 (print) | LCCN 2018027335 (ebook) | ISBN 1620235277 (ebook) | ISBN 9781620235270 (pbk. : alk. paper) | ISBN 9781620235287 (library edition : alk. paper) | ISBN 1620235277 (alk. paper)
Subjects: LCSH: Project Apollo (U.S.)—Juvenile literature. | Apollo 11 (Spacecraft)—Juvenile literature. | Space flight to the moon—Juvenile literature.
Classification: LCC TL789.8.U6 (ebook) | LCC TL789.8.U6 A584375 2018 (print) | DDC 629.45/4—dc23
LC record available at https://lccn.loc.gov/2017057653

Printed in the United States

PROJECT MANAGER: Danielle Lieneman
COVER DESIGN AND INTERIOR LAYOUT: Nicole Sturk

Over the years, we have adopted a number of dogs from rescues and shelters. First there was Bear and after he passed, Ginger and Scout. Now, we have Kira, another rescue. They have brought immense joy and love not just into our lives, but into the lives of all who met them.

We want you to know a portion of the profits of this book will be donated in Bear, Ginger and Scout's memory to local animal shelters, parks, conservation organizations, and other individuals and nonprofit organizations in need of assistance.

– Douglas & Sherri Brown,
President & Vice-President of Atlantic Publishing

TABLE OF CONTENTS

Introduction

THE CHALLENGE

FOUR MONTHS AFTER PRESIDENT JOHN F. KENNEDY'S INAU-guration, he stood before a special joint session of Congress and issued a challenge:

> *"I believe this nation should commit itself to achieving the goal, before this decade is out, of landing a man on the Moon and returning him safely to the Earth."*[1]

There was urgency in the president's message. Why was he eager to send a man to the Moon? It was May 25, 1961, and the United States was already behind in space exploration.

The Soviets — The Union of Soviet Socialist Republics (U.S.S.R.) — were steps ahead of the Americans. The U.S.S.R. was a group of 15 countries (republics) that merged to create one large country. Russia was the largest of these republics. The Soviet Union's capital was Moscow.

When Kennedy was a senator, he'd often criticize his predecessor, President Dwight D. Eisenhower, for his lukewarm response to the Soviets advance-

---

1. NASA, 2013.

ments. As the newly-elected president, the ball was now in Kennedy's court.

The Soviets embarrassed the United States by sending unmanned satellites into space in 1957. The follow-up was equally impressive. On April 12, 1961 Yuri Gagarin became the first human in space.

YURI GAGARIN

Yuri Gagarin on the cover of TIME Magazine on April 21, 1961 following his orbit around the Earth.

Yuri Gagarin was born in Smolensk, Russia in 1934. He moved to Moscow when he was 16 years old. Gagarin initially apprenticed in a metal works shop but quickly transferred to a technical school in Saratov. At his new school, Gagarin joined an aviation club, where he flew for the first time. Gagarin graduated from the Soviet Air Force cadet school and was a fighter pilot. The Soviets selected Gagarin for a special space program in 1960.

On April 12, 1961, Gagarin made one orbit around the Earth, solidifying his place in the history books as the first human in space. Gagarin received the *Order of Lenin*, and his government named him a *Hero of the Soviet Union.*

Gagarin died March 27, 1968 when a fighter jet he was flying, along with fellow cosmonaut, Vladimir Seryogin, crashed near Moscow. The two were participating in a routine training flight. Gagarin was only 34 years old when he died.

It's not that America didn't have her own success stories. On May 5 of the same year, Alan Shepard was the first American to travel to space. His flight was shorter than Gagarin's and it was sub-orbital. While Gagarin orbited once around the Earth, Shepard entered the Earth's atmosphere and then fell back to Earth.

ALAN SHEPARD

Alan Shepard in his spacesuit.

Alan Shepard was one of the original seven astronauts in NASA's Mercury project. Shepard's flight took place only 23 days after Gagarin's space orbit.

Shepard was born November 18, 1923 in Derry, New Hampshire. He joined the U.S. Navy after high school and served in World War II. After the war, he trained as a test pilot. He was also a test pilot school instructor.

The mission launched from sunny Florida, with Shepard aboard the spacecraft *Freedom 7*. He flew 300 miles into outer space during his 15-minute mission. Shepard landed in the Atlantic Ocean, where an aircraft carrier retrieved him. For his accomplishments, Shepard received the *NASA Distinguished Service Medal* from President Kennedy. He also had a huge parade in New York City.

Shepard was eager to return to space but he had an ear problem. Grounded for a decade, he finally returned to space in January 1971. Along with fellow astronaut Ed Mitchell, Shepard blasted to the Moon for the *Apollo 14* mission. The duo spent 33 hours on the Moon. Shepard was the fifth person to walk on the Moon and the first to play golf on the Moon.

Shepard died on July 21, 1998 of leukemia at 74 years old.

PROJECT APOLLO

The president didn't speak to Congress without first investigating the challenges NASA would face during a mission of this magnitude. In April

1961, the president met with an advisory group at the White House to discuss the NASA Space Program. In attendance was:

Jim Webb, NASA administrator

Hugh Dryden, deputy administrator

Ted Sorensen, special counselor

Jerome Wiesner, scientific advisor

David Bell, budget advisor

The president had questions and needed answers before deciding to move forward with the project:

Can the United States catch up to the Soviets?

Can the United States land a man on the Moon before the Soviets?

How much would it cost to land a man on the Moon?

Dryden estimated a cost to be about $40 billion. That's the equivalent of about $330 billion in 2017. The U.S. had a 50/50 chance of a safe Moon landing, he said.

On April 20, President Kennedy sent a memo to Vice President Lyndon B. Johnson, who was also chairman of the Space Council. After Kennedy's advisory meeting, he instructed Johnson to follow up and get the answers he needed.

On April 28, the president received a response from Edward Welsh, Secretary of the National Aeronautics and Space Council (NASC), signed by Johnson. In the memo, Welsh said the survey wasn't complete, but based on preliminary information:

- The Soviets had an advantage over the United States because they started earlier. However, the U.S. government had greater resources than the Soviets. They simply hadn't used the resources effectively.

- Welsh felt the United States could become the world leader in space within the decade.

- Despite the Soviets head start, the United States could catch up — if not surpass — the U.S.S.R.

- If the United States didn't start soon, the window of opportunity would slam on their fingers.

- Other countries would align with the perceived world leader. If the United States reached the Moon first, this would establish the country as the world leader.

- A manned lunar landing was possible in 1966 or 1967.

- The mission would cost approximately $500 million for the fiscal year 1962 in addition to the current budget. Additional funds would help accelerate the program. Welsh estimated that, over a 10-year period, NASA would need about a billion dollars per year in addition to NASA's usual budget.

FAST FACT

National Aeronautics and Space Act of 1958 created NASA:

"To provide for research into problems of flight within and outside the earth's atmosphere, and for other purposes."[2]

---

2. NASA, 2005.

[PUBLIC LAW 85-568]

Eighty-fifth Congress of the United States of America

AT THE SECOND SESSION

Begun and held at the City of Washington on Tuesday, the seventh day of January, one thousand nine hundred and fifty-eight

An Act

To provide for research into problems of flight within and outside the earth's atmosphere, and for other purposes.

Be it enacted by the Senate and House of Representatives of the United States of America in Congress assembled,

TITLE I—SHORT TITLE, DECLARATION OF POLICY, AND DEFINITIONS

SHORT TITLE

Sec. 101. This Act may be cited as the "National Aeronautics and Space Act of 1958".

DECLARATION OF POLICY AND PURPOSE

Sec. 102. (a) The Congress hereby declares that it is the policy of the United States that activities in space should be devoted to peaceful purposes for the benefit of all mankind.

(b) The Congress declares that the general welfare and security of the United States require that adequate provision be made for aeronautical and space activities. The Congress further declares that such activities shall be the responsibility of, and shall be directed by, a civilian agency exercising control over aeronautical and space activities sponsored by the United States, except that activities peculiar to or primarily associated with the development of weapons systems, military operations, or the defense of the United States (including the research and development necessary to make effective provision for the defense of the United States) shall be the responsibility of, and shall be directed by, the Department of Defense; and that determination as to which such agency has responsibility for and direction of any such activity shall be made by the President in conformity with section 201 (e).

(c) The aeronautical and space activities of the United States shall be conducted so as to contribute materially to one or more of the following objectives:

(1) The expansion of human knowledge of phenomena in the atmosphere and space;

(2) The improvement of the usefulness, performance, speed, safety, and efficiency of aeronautical and space vehicles;

(3) The development and operation of vehicles capable of carrying instruments, equipment, supplies, and living organisms through space;

(4) The establishment of long-range studies of the potential benefits to be gained from, the opportunities for, and the problems involved in the utilization of aeronautical and space activities for peaceful and scientific purposes;

(5) The preservation of the role of the United States as a leader in aeronautical and space science and technology and in the application thereof to the conduct of peaceful activities within and outside the atmosphere;

(6) The making available to agencies directly concerned with national defense of discoveries that have military value or significance, and the furnishing by such agencies, to the civilian agency established to direct and control nonmilitary aeronautical and space activities, of information as to discoveries which have value or significance to that agency;

The Space Act of 1958.

Armed with this information and a driving desire to position the United States as world leader, President Kennedy spoke to Congress and the nation.

Kennedy acknowledged the Soviet's recent accomplishments. He mentioned he had been reviewing the space program since taking office and shared with Congress the results of the preliminary report.

The U.S. government had the resources and the talent to perform a successful lunar mission. The president said past leadership wasn't strong. "We have never specified long range goals on an urgent time schedule, or managed our resources and our time so as to ensure their fulfillment."[3]

The Soviets had several months lead time. Should the United States give up space exploration? Not only should NASA not give up, Kennedy said, but they should increase their effort. "For while we cannot guarantee that we shall one day be first, we can guarantee that any failure to make this effort will find us last."[4]

The idea of space exploration was no longer a distant dream but a close reality, thanks to the Soviets. But this didn't mean the U.S. shouldn't move forward to explore instead of relying on second-hand information.

The project was exciting and important for the space exploration program. But Kennedy admitted the road ahead was difficult *and* expensive.

The president proposed to accelerate the development of a lunar spacecraft and to develop alternative liquid and solid fuel boosters. He requested money to fund engine development and for unmanned explorations, emphasizing the importance of performing an unmanned exploration first.

3. NASA, 2013.
4. NASA, 2013.

The United States had to be sure they could land a man on the moon *and* return him safely to earth. "But in a real sense, it will not be one man going to the moon — it will be an entire nation. For all of us must work to put him there," he said.[5]

How much would the program cost? Here's a breakdown of what the president requested:

- $23 million — in addition to $7 million already earmarked — to fast-track the development of the ROVER nuclear rocket engine program

- $50 million for space satellite communication development

- $75 million — $53 million going to the Weather Bureau for development of a new weather satellite system.

"Let it be clear that I am asking the Congress and the country to accept a firm commitment to a new course of action — A course which will last for many years and carry very heavy cost ... " [6]

Having enough money to move forward wasn't enough to achieve success. Kennedy added: "This decision demands a major national commitment of scientific and technical manpower, material and facilities ... "[7]

The project needed dedicated, organized, and disciplined people. Kennedy cautioned that the program couldn't afford " ... undue work stoppages, inflated costs of material or talent, wasteful interagency rivalries, or hot turnover of key personnel."[8]

---

5. NASA, 2013.
6. NASA, 2013.
7. NASA, 2013.
8. NASA, 2013.

FAST FACT

On August 7, Congress approved $1.67 billion budget for NASA.

Could the United States send a man to the Moon and return him safely to Earth? No one knew for sure. They were treading on unfamiliar territory. There wasn't a guidebook. *They* would have to write the manual. Eager men and women accepted the president's challenge and became part of the mission to send a man to the Moon. This is their story as much as it is the tale of three *Apollo 11* astronauts who made it to the Moon and returned safely to Earth.

PRESIDENT JOHN F. KENNEDY

John Fitzgerald Kennedy, the 35th president of the United States.

President John Fitzgerald Kennedy (JFK) was the 35th president of the United States. Kennedy was born in Brookline, New York in 1917. He served in the Navy, after graduating from Harvard in 1940. Returning from the Navy in 1945, Kennedy began his political career. He served as a member of the U.S. House of Representatives (1947-1953) and as a senator (1953-1960) before setting his sights on Pennsylvania Ave. He was inaugurated January 20, 1961.

Unfortunately, Kennedy wouldn't live to see the first moonwalk. Lee Harvey Oswald assassinated Kennedy in Dallas, Texas on November 22, 1963.

Chapter 1

RACE TO SPACE

YURI GAGARIN DIDN'T JUST JUMP IN A SPACE CAPSULE AND *zoom* into outer space. Neither did Alan Shepard. The Soviets and the United States' unmanned missions tested the ability to send humans into orbit. This chapter discusses these early missions. But first we look at the impetus for the United States' drive to land a man on the Moon — The Cold War.

--- *FAST FACT* ---

What is outer space? Scientists define outer space as any space 62.5 miles above the surface of the Earth.

THE COLD WAR

The rivalry between the United States and the Soviet Union didn't always exist. During World War II, both fought as allies against the Axis powers (Germany, Italy, and Japan). Fighting together, though, didn't make the two countries pals. The countries' relationship to each other was lukewarm but not openly confrontational.

Let's call them *frenemies*. In fact, although "frenemy" seems like a recent term, journalist Walter Winchell coined the term in 1953. "Howz about calling the Russians our Frenemies?" he asked in his syndicated column. [9]

The United States didn't like the Soviets' Communist government. There was growing concern about the Russian leader Joseph Stalin; many Americans thought he was a tyrant. And on the other side, there was resentment from the Soviets because America refused to acknowledge the U.S.S.R. as a legitimate government and for the United States' late entry into World War II. Some Russians blamed the U.S. government's slow response for the death of many Soviet citizens during the war.

After the war, the two countries started openly chatting about their mutual distrust. When the Soviet Union expanded into Eastern Europe, many Americans feared that the Russians were trying to take over the world.

This began the Cold War. The Cold War refers to the icy relationship between the two countries rather than outright military action. The U.S. government felt the best way to deal with the Soviet Union was containment, which involved stopping the Soviets from expanding their influence.

In the Soviet Union, the government operated as a communist dictatorship, controlling every aspect of a citizen's life. Individuals couldn't own property or run their own business. The society was classless in that the distribution of wealth was equal. The government provided free healthcare and education, but they also controled the press.

The United States, however, is the opposite, it operates on the concept of capitalism. Citizens live in a democratic society and control their own wealth. They are free to work the jobs they want or start their own busi-

---

9. Purcell, 2016.

nesses. In a capitalistic society, the result of labor belongs wholly to the citizen who labored. The press is free to write whatever they choose. Citizens are responsible for the cost of their own healthcare and educational needs (with government assistance, if necessary).

FAST FACT

Writer George Orwell, author of *1984* and *Animal Farm,* was the first to use the term "cold war" to refer to the post-War tension between the United States and the U.S.S.R. The term appeared in an essay Orwell wrote in 1945, titled "You and the Atomic Bomb".

George Orwell, author of 1984 *and* Animal Farm.

The Cold War also signaled the start of the Arms Race. This was a time when both governments aspired to create superior military arms or weapons. The U.S. government vowed to stop communist expansion. Could atomic weapons — like the ones that ended World War II — be the solution to winning the Arms Race?

In 1949, the Soviets begin testing atomic bombs. In retaliation, President Harry S. Truman said the United States would build a bigger and more destructive weapon: the hydrogen bomb. Stalin said they would also build a hydrogen bomb. The U.S. government and the Soviet Union began testing these destructive and poisonous missiles.

Both the United States and Soviets next turned their eyes to the sky — literally. Each country wanted to be the first to travel outside Earth's atmosphere. When the Soviets sprinted over the first hurdle, slow and steady wins the Space Race. The Cold War didn't end when the *Apollo 11* astronauts walked on the Moon, but continued on for decades.

Most of the problems between the U.S. and the Soviet Union revolved around one issue: communism. Still, the U.S. government attempted to build a better relationship with the Soviets. They also wanted to erase the constant threat of nuclear war.

In 1972, President Richard Nixon — along with Soviet Premier Leonid Brezhnev — signed *The Strategic Arms Limitation Treaty (Salt 1)*. The premier was the head of the U.S.S.R.'s government. By signing the treaty, both countries agreed to not manufacture nuclear missiles. They also agreed to cease the constant threats of nuclear war.

However, the Cold War *still* wasn't over. When President Ronald Reagan took office in the 1980s, he asked the government to provide financial and military aid to freedom fighters combating communism. Reagan felt communism was spreading like a bad rash, calling it a global threat. Reagan named his foreign aid policy, *The Reagan Doctrine*.

Fortunately for the U.S., the Soviet Union was crumbling on its own. In 1985 the new premier — Mikhail Gorbachev — instituted new policies that affected the way Soviets interacted with the rest of the political world.

In 1989, the remaining Soviet states replaced their government with a non-communist one, and in November, the Berlin Wall fell, bringing down the last symbol of the Cold War. The wall, built in 1961, was a barrier designed to keep Germans from escaping communist East Berlin into democratic West Berlin. After World War II ended, Germany split into four blocs or zones: Soviet, American, British, and French. Berlin was part of the Soviet zone; however, it split into East (communist) and West (democratic) Berlin. West Germany provided better opportunities to her citizens, who fled the country in record numbers. The wall was an attempt to keep East German citizens from fleeing.

In 1987, President Reagan famously uttered the words, "Mr. Gorbachev, tear down this wall!" [10]

The Cold War officially ended in 1991. The Soviet Union had collapsed.

EARLY SPACE MISSIONS

Now that we know the catalyst for the space race, let's look at some of the early missions.

October 4, 1957: *The Soviets launched Sputnik 1.* The race to space between the Soviets and the United States began October 4, 1957. We learned in the introduction that on this day the unmanned satellite *Sputnik 1* launched into space. The satellite was a metal ball with four, 10 foot long radio antennas poking out from the side.

Sputnik orbited the Earth once every 96 minutes, transmitting a radio signal as it traveled. Amateur radio operators easily picked up the signal. With the right pair of binoculars, many below could view *Sputnik* from their backyard. The satellite made 1,400 orbits before re-entering the Earth's atmosphere and burning up on January 4, 1958.

---

10. Robinson, 2007.

A replica of Sputnik 1 *located at the U.S. National Air and Space Museum.*

November 3, 1957: *The Soviets launched Sputnik 2.* The Soviets followed their first launch by sending a dog named Laika into space a month later. The United States and the U.S.S.R. routinely used animals to tests the effects of weightlessness in space. Scientists hoped to better understand how space atmosphere might affect humans by studying the dog. Laika was a mixed breed (primarily Siberian Husky) rescue dog.

FAST FACT

Laika's original name was "Kudryavka," the Russian word for several breeds of dog like a husky. American reporters nicknamed her "Muttnik".

Unfortunately, Laika didn't make it back to Earth. The power to her life support system gave out. Scientists aren't sure exactly how long she lived while in space. *Sputnik 2* ignited in the Earth's upper atmosphere in April 1958.

December 6, 1957: *Vanguard TV-3*. The U.S. government tried unsuccessfully to send the *Vanguard* satellite into space. After rising only four feet into the air, the satellite plummeted back to the ground where it exploded. The Soviet newspapers mocked the United States' efforts. They called the satellite *Dudnik* and *Kaputnik*.

Explosion of the Vanguard TV-3.

January 31, 1958: The United States launched *Explorer 1*. This satellite carried instruments to study cosmic rays. While in space, it discovered the Van Allen radiation belt — a doughnut-shaped region around the Earth filled with charged particles trapped by the Earth's magnetic field. Radio transmission stopped in May 1958, but the satellite remained in space until 1970. After completing 58,000 orbits around the Earth, the satellite burned up in the atmosphere.

March 17, 1958: The United States launched *Vanguard 1*. Unleashed on St. Patrick's Day, the *Vanguard 1* satellite stopped transmitting in April 1964. It's still circling the Earth (as of February 2018) and is the oldest artificial satellite in space.

October 11, 1958: The United States launched *Pioneer 1*. This was the first spacecraft launched after the formation of NASA. Its mission was to survey the space environment near Earth and the Moon. It didn't reach the Moon but managed to transmit data back to NASA scientists.

January 2, 1959: The Soviets launched *Luna 1*. While the probe didn't successfully make it to the Moon, the unmanned spacecraft was the first to leave Earth's atmosphere (escape Earth's gravitational pull) and was also the first spacecraft to orbit the Sun.

February 17, 1959: The United States launched *Vanguard 2*. The satellite's mission was to measure cloud-cover distribution. Because of issues at liftoff, the satellite "wobbled." This resulted in poor data transmission. One transmitter continued to send data for 23 days and another for 26. Then the batteries fizzled out. The *Vanguard 1* is still orbiting. Scientists say it could continue circling for 200-300 years!

February 28, 1959: The United States launched *Discoverer 1*. The purpose of this spacecraft was to spy on the Soviet Union. The satellite's mission was to transmit photographic images of that showed whether the Soviets were producing and deploying long-range missiles. The true reason for the mission was kept quiet until 1995 when the government declassified the programs' documents.

The Discoverer 1 *was intended to spy on the Soviet Union.*

March 3, 1959: The United States launched *Pioneer 4*. The government launched the *Pioneer 4* spacecraft hoping to get photographs of the Moon. The spacecraft whizzed by the Moon, but because of errors in planning the trajectory, the camera's sensor didn't trigger. *Pioneer's* radio transmitted value data for 82 hours before scientists lost contact with the object March 6, 1959.

May 28, 1959: NASA sent two monkeys into space. The primates, named Able and Baker (both females), survived the flight. Unfortunately, Able died four days after returning to our planet. She had a fatal reaction to anesthesia administered during surgery to remove an electrode. Baker died in 1984 at 27 years old.

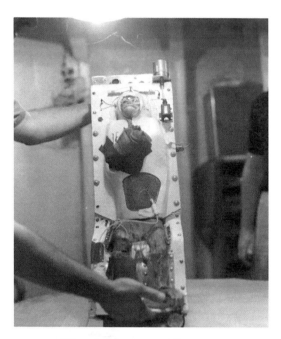

Able, after she returned from space.

June 25, 1959: The United States attempted to launch *Discoverer 4* — another spy satellite — but it failed to lift off.

March 5, 1958; August 24, 1958: The United States tried unsuccessfully to launch *Explorer 2* and *Explorer 5* satellites before the successful launch of *Explorer 6*.

August 7, 1959: The U.S. government launched *Explorer 6*. This research satellite provided the first grainy pictures of Earth, taken from space.

September 12, 1959: The Soviets launched *Luna 2*. Two days after the launch, the Soviets intentionally crashed *Luna* on the Moon.

September 17, 1959: NASA tested the extremely fast X-15 hypersonic research plane.

October 4, 1959: The Soviets launched *Luna 3*. The Luna spacecraft was the third to reach the Moon and the first to send back images of the far side of the Moon. *Luna 3* stopped transmitting on October 22. Scientist speculate the probe baked in Earth's atmosphere in March or April 1960. However, it's possible it continued to orbit until 1962.

FAST FACT

Television Infrared Observation Satellite Program (*TIROS*) was the United States' first weather satellite. Launched April 1, 1960, it transmitted data for only 78 days but proved satellites could provide useful information on weather conditions from space.

August 10, 1960: NASA launched *Discoverer 13*. In this mission, NASA recovered the first man-made object from orbit. The satellite contained a telemetry system, tape recorder, receiver, scanner, and a 120-lb recovery capsule. Inside the capsule was an American flag. On August 11, the command center sent a message to the satellite to begin the recovery sequence. The mission was successful. President Eisenhower received the recovered flag on August 15.

August 10, 1960: The United States launched *Echo,* a communications satellite. *Echo* was a balloon satellite that inflated in space.

August 1960: The U.S. launched *Discoverer 14*. Part of the spy satellite program, *Discoverer 14*, was the first successful low-resolution spacecraft. This mission was the first successful recovery of film from an orbiting object. It was also the first successful aerial or mid-air recovery of an object returning from Earth's orbit.

August 1960: The Soviets launched *Sputnik 5*. This mission tested the feasibility of a manned journey. The Soviets didn't use men, though. They sent two dogs into space — Belka and Strelka. Both animals returned to Earth safely after a one-day mission.

A 50ᵗʰ anniversary stamp in Russia commemorating the two dogs that went into space, Belka and Strelka.

As you read in the introduction, Yuri Gagarin, and Alan Shepard, became the first men in space in 1961, setting in motion a more urgent need for the U.S. or the Soviets to reach the Moon first. On the heels of President Kennedy's impassioned speech and the creation of NASA, the United States stepped up its efforts.

Chapter 2

ASTRONAUT SELECTION AND TRAINING

LANDING A MAN ON THE MOON INVOLVED A SERIES OF OR-chestrated exercises. Think of the missions as steps on the rungs of a ladder. Before the Apollo project, there was Mercury and Gemini. These early projects were the lower and middle rungs of the ladder. The upper rungs represent the early Apollo missions. The top rung was *Apollo 11*.

At this point, maybe you're wondering how NASA selected and trained the astronauts for these early missions.

PROJECT MERCURY: SELECTION

As NASA prepared to "race to space," there was something missing. They needed men to complete the missions. They needed astronauts. In October 1958, NASA began recruiting for the space project named "Mercury." They needed seven men to complete seven missions.

Many who came were daredevils and those seeking adventure. Some were racecar drivers and mountain climbers. NASA rejected most of the men who answered the call. They weren't the type of men NASA had in mind.

NASA wanted men trained in aeronautics. They wanted "... stable, college-educated test pilots screened for mental difficulties ..."[11]

NASA also wanted military test pilots for this landmark venture. Specific requirements were:

1. **Age:** *younger than 40*

2. **Height:** *5 feet 11 inches or shorter*

3. **Weight:** *less than 180 pounds*

4. **Health:** *in excellent physical condition*

5. **Education:** *Bachelor's degree (preferably in Engineering)*

6. **Pilot experience:** *graduate of a test-pilot school; 1,500 hours of flying time; qualified as a jet pilot*

FAST FACT: NO GIRLS ALLOWED

There were no women candidates, not because NASA prohibited them from applying but because there were no female military test pilots during this time period.

Hundreds of men sprinted to NASA to volunteer for the program. Here's a numbers breakdown of the selection process:

- A committee evaluated **500+** applicants

- They selected **110** to interview

- **32** received second interviews and testing (including psychological evaluations)

11. Barbree, 2014.

Testing the candidates

NASA would choose seven from the finalists. The U.S. government was ready for space flight, but no one knew the effects of space travel on the human body. The doctors who examined the volunteers subjected them to many tests.

NASA tested the applicants in clusters — five groups of six men each and one group with two men. For the physical examinations, the volunteers travelled to the Lovelace Clinic in Albuquerque, New Mexico. Working with one group at a time, the testing lasted 7 ½ days per group. Doctors tested in six categories:

1. **History, aviation, and medical:** routine medical examinations given to the candidate under normal conditions, after he's has had time to rest; information on the applicant's flying history/number of hours logged; and a detailed family medical history.

2. **Physical examination:** additional head-to-toe examinations including testing of eyes, ears, and heart functions. The candidates received a neurological exam that tested reflexes and coordination.

3. **Laboratory tests:** numerous blood and urine tests including blood count, fasting blood sugar level, cholesterol and sodium levels, a throat culture, and fecal stool examination.

4. **Radiographic examinations:** x-rays of the teeth, sinuses, thorax, esophagus, stomach, colon, and spine; a cardiogram of the heart.

5. **Physical competence and ventilatory efficiency tests:** tested the candidate's overall physical and cardiopulmonary (heart and lung) capacity.

6. **Final evaluation:** a final summary — based on results of all test — focused on the candidate's physical, mental, and social well-being.

Stress testing

The Air Force Research and Development Command conducted the next phase of testing. An investigator from the Physical Fitness Test Unit and the Psychology Test Unit administered the examinations in Dayton, Ohio.

Most of the assessments wouldn't raise an eyebrow — walking on a tread-mill to measure physical agility — for example. But some of the tests were ... *unusual.* For example: How many balloons could candidate blow up before he collapsed? Other exams included:

- **The cold pressor:** The applicant plunged his feet into a tub of ice-cold water.

- **Isolation:** Applicant sits in a dark, soundproof room for three hours.

- **Heat:** Can you imagine sitting in a 130-degree room for two hours? This was one of the stress tests the would-be astronauts faced.

During this phase, the candidates also endured 25 psychological tests. One test asked the men to write 20 answers to the question: *Who am I?*

FAST FACT

The word "astronaut" comes from Greek, meaning "space sailor." Russian astronauts are "cosmonauts".

Final evaluation and selection

After all testing was complete, a team met at Langley, NASA's Research Center in Virginia. The group included representatives from NASA, the

U. S. Air Force Aerospace Medical Laboratory, and the Lovelace Foundation. They would collectively decide the fate of the "32."

April 2, 1959, NASA announced the Mercury Seven:

Walter "Wally" Schirra   *Alan Shepard*

Donald "Deke" Slayton   *Virgil "Gus" Grissom*

John Glenn   *L. Gordon Cooper*

M. Scott Carpenter

Carpenter/Cooper/Glenn/Grissom/Schirra/Shepard/Slayton

*A collage of the Project Mercury mission
including the astronauts, rockets, and spacecraft.*

——— **FAST FACT** ———————————————————

The Mercury 7's IQs ranged from 130 to 145, with an average of 136. They were all men with superior intelligence. The average IQ score for most people is in the 85-115 range.

As you continue reading, you'll notice Mercury completed six manned missions. Why only six when there were seven Mercury astronauts, though? An irregular heart beat sidelined Deke Slayton. NASA scrapped the mission because they had already completed the Mercury objectives and were ready to move on, in any case. Slayton would still play an important part at NASA, but more about his role later.

PROJECT MERCURY: TRAINING

The trainees spent their days going back and forth between the classroom and physical training for space flight. A big part of training took place in simulators. These machines fell into two categories: the kinds that mimicked what an astronaut might experience in space (weightlessness, for example) and devices that allowed astronauts to practice space flight. One of the most famous training devices was fondly nicknamed "The Vomit Comet."

The Vomit Comet

The Vomit Comet was a Boeing KC-135 aircraft used to simulate the experience of anti-gravity. The plane would soar into the air and then take a sharp dive into a parabolic arc to create a zero-gravity experience. The astronauts would then float inside the cabin for about 15 seconds. This experience often made the trainees literally vomit, resulting in the nickname for the simulation.

Survival Training

What would happen if the worst-case scenario occurred and astronauts had to bail out of the craft? A problem could arise any time after lift-off. To plan for emergencies, astronauts underwent hardcore survival training.

FAST FACT

Survival training took place in Panama at the U.S. Air Force tropical survival school.

If something went wrong with the flight, the astronauts could end up anywhere. Strong possibilities included bodies of water, remote islands, or a desert. Survival suits are standard on each spacecraft.

During one training exercise, astronauts are "marooned" in the jungle for days to practice their survival skills in the event that they become temporarily stranded in such a place after bailing out.

SURVIVAL CLASSES

So what type of survival classes did the astronauts take? Here's a sample course schedule:

Tent Making 101: *How to make a tent with your parachute if you're stranded in the desert.*

Jungle Cuisine for Beginners: *How to kill and eat a snake (before he kills and eats you!) if you're trapped in the jungles of Panama.*

It's Getting Hot in Here: *How to not get burned by volcanic lava in Hawaii.*

(*Okay*, we may have made up the names of the classes, but the training was real!)

Each astronaut received a survival manual with helpful tips. Are you trying to figure out what's safe to eat? No problem: "Anything that creeps, crawls, swims, or flies is a possible source of food." [12]

For those shaking their heads saying they would *never* eat an insect, the manual added this cheery note: "You have probably eaten insects as con-taminants in flour, corn meal, rice, beans, fruits, and greens of your daily food, and in stores in general." [13] In other words, you've probably already munched on bugs and haven't known it, so you can certainly do it again in order to survive. It then goes on to explain which bugs are best to eat and how to cook them.

The handbook offered tips on catching (and cooking) wild pigs, porcu-pines, deer, and ... monkeys. *Sorry, George!*

"But I'm a vegetarian!" you scream.

No problem — the handy guide offered choices for vegetarians, instruct-ing astronauts on how to cook taro and other vegetation. But if you see a wild mushroom growing, don't gobble it up because you can't tell the poi-sonous ones simply by a funky odor or taste.

Other survival tips included remedies for stinging creatures like wasps and how to handle scorpions and snakes.

Suppose astronauts become stranded on an inhabited island on which the natives don't speak English. According to the survival manual, you shouldn't "... be afraid to be an object of amusement to the natives." [14]

---

12. Collins, 1974.
13. Collins, 1974.
14. Collins, 1974.

Say what now? That's right, the men should "Be ready to entertain with songs, games, or tricks of cards, coins, or strings ..." [15] Next, negotiate with items like rock salt and tobacco, *but not paper money.* Whip out the Benjamins only if necessary and "discreetly" during trading sessions. Finally, "State your business simply and frankly."[16] Then cross your fingers someone understands the words flowing from your mouth.

And just in case the astronauts felt like behaving badly, the manual warned them to "... ***leave the native women alone at all times***" while waiting for rescue. [17]

The manual assured the men that if they became stranded, they should tell fear to take a hike. "You are probably safer from sudden death in the jungle than in most big cities," it read.[18]

The astronauts worked in pairs, performing tasks like hiking from the drop-off spot to locate their assigned camping area. The men had to make hammocks and search for food. Sometimes they would meet natives (pre-arranged) and practice their communication and trade skills.

The jungle wasn't the only survival location. The sweltering Nevada desert served as training facility, as well. There, the astronauts had two primary tasks:

1. Learn how to conserve body fluids, and

2. Learn how to signal for help

---

15. Collins, 1974.
16. Collins, 1974.
17. Collins, 1974.
18. Collins, 1974.

PROJECT MERCURY: MISSIONS OVERVIEW

Alan Shepard's May 1961 suborbital flight was the first of the Mercury missions. Shephard's flight onboard *Freedom 7* paved the way for Virgil "Gus" Grissom to make a second manned suborbital flight on July 21, 1961. The *Liberty Bell 7's* 15 minutes, 37 second mission was 9 seconds longer than Shepard's.

On February 20, 1961, John Glenn achieved another milestone for the United States. His mission onboard *Friendship 7* became the first manned orbital flight. The duration of his mission was just under five hours.

JOHN GLENN

John Glenn was born in Cambridge, Ohio on July 18, 1921. His family moved to New Concord, Ohio when Glenn was toddler. After graduating high school in 1939, Glenn enrolled in Muskingum College. In 1942, he enlisted in the Naval Aviation Cadet Program. In 1943, he became a Marine fighter pilot, flying 59 combat missions in the South Pacific during World War II.

Glenn also served as a pilot during the Korean War. After the war, Glenn enrolled in the U.S. Navy Test Pilot School in Maryland. In 1957, he set a speed record for traveling from coast to coast (Los Angeles to New York) in three hours, 23 minutes.

In 1959, Glenn made the roster of the *Mercury 7*. He would glide into the history books as the first to man to orbit Earth.

The government showered Glenn with parades and awards when he returned from his outer space adventure. Among the awards he received was the NASA Distinguished Service Medal. He remained at NASA until 1964.

In 1965, he retired from the Marines Corps and entered politics. His political career stalled because of injuries sustained in an accident. He took a job at Royal Crown Cola, serving as vice-president and then president. In 1970, he jumped back into the political ring. He ran for a U.S. Senate seat but didn't win. He didn't give up, though, a won a seat in 1974. Glenn served four terms in Congress, retiring from the Senate in 1999. He considered running for president in 1984, but withdrew from the race during the primaries.

Glenn was the first man to orbit the Earth *and* the oldest man in space. On October 29, 1998, Glenn was on the crew of the *Discovery* space shuttle. He was 77. Part of the nine-day mission was to investigate the effects on aging during space travel. Glenn died December 8, 2016 at the age of 95.

M. Scott Carpenter followed Glenn's mission on *Aurora 7*, for the second manned orbital flight on May 24, 1962. His mission lasted just under five hours. Walter Schirra nearly doubled the length of the two previous missions, his lasting 9 hours, 13 minutes, and 11 seconds. He orbited twice as many times as Glenn and Carpenter during his *Sigma 7* mission.

The last of the *Mercury* missions launched May 15, 1963. *Faith 7*, with L. Gordon Cooper at the control, was the first day-long mission. The duration was 1 day, 10 hours, 19 minutes, and 49 seconds.

PROJECT GEMINI: SELECTION AND TRAINING

When it was time for NASA to find the second group of astronauts, they still wanted military test pilots. The project would mimic many of the situations an astronaut might face during a lunar mission. It was imperative the men chosen for the project could pull off these critical maneuvers. NASA had specific traits in mind.

They wanted someone who was:

- Comfortable in dangerous situations

- Able to make quick reactions in emergencies

- Highly intelligent

- Able to learn new, complex systems/technologies

- In excellent health

Remember Deke Slayton? When NASA grounded Deke Slayton, he remained with the agency in a very important managerial position. Deke was responsible for choosing the astronauts for the Gemini and Apollo missions and oversaw the training of the astronauts.

DONALD "DEKE" SLAYTON

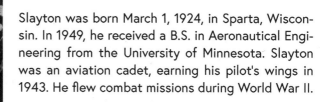

Donald "Deke" Slayton

Slayton was born March 1, 1924, in Sparta, Wisconsin. In 1949, he received a B.S. in Aeronautical Engineering from the University of Minnesota. Slayton was an aviation cadet, earning his pilot's wings in 1943. He flew combat missions during World War II.

In 1955, Slayton enrolled in the United States Air Force Test Pilot School at Edwards Air Force Base in California and was a test pilot at the base for three years (1956-59).

Slayton became Coordinator of Astronaut Activities in September 1962. This critical position made him responsible for the day-to-day operation of the astronaut office. He became Director of Flight Crew Operations in November 1963 which meant that he'd oversee the activities of the astronaut office, the aircraft operations office, the flight crew integration division, the crew training and simulation division, and the crew procedures division.

Slayton eventually got the chance to take a space flight. In July 1975, he participated a joint docking test mission. The Apollo-Soyuz Test Project (ASTP) mission was the first meeting in space between U.S. astronauts and Soviet cosmonauts.

Slayton worked at NASA until his retirement in 1982. He died June 13, 1993 of a brain tumor.

Volunteers endured the same physical and psychological tests as the Mercury candidates. On September 17, 1962 NASA announced the new astronauts.

The "New Nine" Astronauts of the Gemini Project:

James McDivitt   *Frank Borman*

James Lovell   *Neil Armstrong*

Ed White   *John Young*

Thomas Stafford   *Elliot See*

Charles Conrad

FAST FACT

James Lovell and Charles Conrad were candidates for Project Mercury, but they flunked the tests.

Along with Mercury veteran astronauts — Grissom, Cooper, Shirra, and Shepard — the Gemini astronauts were ready to further explore space.

The new trainees arrived on the tail end of the Mercury project. This gave them an opportunity to see first-hand how to prepare for a mission. Classroom, simulator, and real-world scenarios continued. The Gemini men would be responsible for flight maneuvers and testing the procedures that would ensure a successful lunar landing.

PROJECT GEMINI: MISSIONS OVERVIEW

The Gemini Program completed ten missions in 1965 and 1966. Each mission lasted a day or longer, with two exceptions, and every mission was a two-man flight. On March 23, 1965 Gus Grissom returned to space with John Young on the first Gemini mission (*Gemini 3*). The first mission lasted just under five hours.

A patch from the Project Gemini mission.

Gemini 4 launched on June 3, 1965, carrying James McDivitt and Edward White into space for four days. Their mission was the first multi-day flight and the first spacewalk by U.S. astronauts.

L. Gordon Cooper and Charles "Pete" Conrad, took *Gemini 5* on a week-long space excursion. Launched on August 21, 1965, the crew returned August 29.

Frank Borman and James Lovell's mission lasted 13 days. They hold the world record for the spaceflight of longest duration. *Gemini 7* launched on December 4, 1965 and returned December 18.

Gemini 6-A was a day-long mission with Walter Schirra and Thomas Stafford as crew members. It launched December 14. *Gemini 6-A* and *Gemini 7* was the first orbital rendezvous — the two spacecrafts met in space.

Neil Armstrong and David Scott's 10-hour mission was the second Mercury flight that lasted under one day. The *Gemini 8* launched March 16, 1966. It was the first space docking test, but because of problems with the spacecraft, they had to scrap the remainder of the mission.

Gemini 9-A was a 3-day, 21-hour mission that launched on June 3, 1966 with astronauts Thomas Stafford and Eugene Cernan.

The first double rendezvous and two spacewalks happened during the *Gemini 10* mission. John Young and Michael Collins left Earth on July 18, 1966, returning July 21.

Charles "Pete" Conrad and Richard Gordon flew *Gemini 11*. The mission lasted just under three days, launching September 12, 1966. This mission was the first to have computer-controlled re-entry.

The last Gemini mission (*Gemini 12*) launched November 11, 1966 and returned November 15 with crew members James Lovell and Edwin "Buzz" Aldrin. During this last mission there were three spacewalks.

PROJECT APOLLO: SELECTION

When it was time to select volunteers for the Apollo project, many of the tests from previous missions had been retired, but a few strange ones were still used. For example, one test pumped icy water into candidates' ears for an extended period of time. Candidates still sat in dark, soundproof rooms, but for two hours now, instead of three. One test placed candidates in a scorching hot room with temperatures that rose as high as 145 degrees Fahrenheit. In one test, they even had to sit on a block of ice and whistle while eating crackers. NASA *did* dropp the test pilot requirement, though.

Were all of the the tests really necessary? That was a question many astronauts asked. They argued some tests were not space-related. Was NASA using the candidates as human guinea pigs for medical doctors? No one knows for sure, but some of the men certainly thought they were.

Here's how astronaut Michael Collins described the physical exams: "Inconvenience is piled on top of uncertainty on top of indignity, as you are poked, prodded, pummeled, and pierced. You are a secondhand car being inspected prior to a coast-to-coast trip." [19]

One of the more reasonable tests placed volunteers flat on their backs on a table. Suddenly the table jerks upright. This test measured the men's cardiovascular response to sudden shifts in gravity.

Psychological evaluations continued, as well. "Are you a snob or a slob?" one asked. [20] Others asked the men to describe what they saw on a blank, white sheet of paper.

On October 17, 1963, NASA announced their selection, usually called "The Fourteen." The class of 1963 brought the number of NASA astronauts to 30.

---

19. Collins, 1974.
20. Collins, 1974.

"The Fourteen" Astronauts were:

Edwin "Buzz" Aldrin	*Clifton Williams*
David Scott	*Michael Collins*
William Anders	*R. Walter Cunningham*
Charles Bassett	*Donn Eisele*
Alan Bean	*Theodore Freeman*
Eugene Cernan	*Richard Gordon*
Roger Chaffee	*Russell Schweickart*

FAST FACT

Elliot See and Charlie Bassett died February 28, 1966 when their T-38 trainer jet crashed into the side of a building in St. Louis. Neither had the chance to complete their scheduled mission.

PROJECT APOLLO: TRAINING

The astronauts trained in simulators as the Mercury and Gemini crew before them. They also practiced situations that would be useful during a lunar mission. For example, they practiced collecting rock samples and drove moon buggies over a mock lunar surface.

Many tests were like full dress rehearsals. The astronauts wore pressurized suits while *galumphing* along loaded down with cumbersome backpacks.

The new astronauts also trained in the classroom. They studied astronomy and aerodynamics. They logged hours learning about rocket propulsion and meteorology. Geology, communications, and flight mechanics were also on the syllabus.

Because the spacecraft relied heavily on computer navigation, the crew also received 36 hours of digital computer training.

The astronauts' training also included field trips. It was one thing to examine rocks in a classroom setting, but seeing hundreds of formations in the Grand Canyon was a totally unique experience.

PROJECT APOLLO: EARLY MISSIONS OVERVIEW

The Apollo spacecrafts consisted of three modules, or parts, launched by a Saturn rocket.

1. **The Command Module (CM)** was where the astronauts lived during the flight. The CM attached to the service module.

2. **The Service Module** housed propulsion, electrical power, and life support systems.

3. **The Lunar Module (LM — pronounced "LEM")** was the craft in which two of the astronauts would descend to the Moon. The third astronaut would remain in the command module and orbit the Moon.

Apollo 1

Edward White, Virgil "Gus" Grissom, and Roger Chaffee, were excited about being the first crew scheduled to orbit the Earth in the new Apollo program. The scheduled launch date was February 21. Unfortunately, tragedy struck on January 27, 1967. While conducting a routine training test, the spacecraft caught fire and the three astronauts died in the blazing accident.

The crew of Apollo 1(from left to right): Gus Grissom, Ed White, and Roger Chaffee.

The crew was participating in a "plugs-out" test. In this scenario, NASA mounted the CM on the on the (unfueled) Saturn rocket launcher, as it would be for the real launch in February. The crew would simulate the countdown sequence, stopping short of the actual launch.

Everything was going according to plan except that the radio wasn't working properly. "How are we going to go to the Moon, if we can't talk between three buildings?" Grissom asked. [21]

Then something went horribly wrong. Over the radio, command center heard a terrifying sentence.

---

21. Pyle, 2005.

"I smell fire," Chaffee said. [22]

Two seconds later, White screamed, "Fire in the cockpit!" [23]

Within seconds the men were dead. The door hatch to the CM opened only from the inside. Normally, it took about 90 seconds to get the door open because of all the latches or bolts holding the door secure, but the fire spread too quickly. The men didn't have a chance.

Technicians managed to open the hatch, but it took five minutes. The astronauts had probably died from severe burns and smoke inhalation within the first 30 seconds of the fire starting.

An investigation pinpointed the start of the fire from a spark from faulty wiring under Grissom's chair. The cabin was ripe with flammable material. These factors, combined with the oxygen-rich environment, made the Command Module a tinderbox waiting to catch.

FAST FACT

Apollo 1 was actually officially named Apollo 204, but most people at NASA called the mission Apollo 1. After the astronauts' deaths, the government officially renamed the mission Apollo 1 to honor the fallen crew.

NASA made some changes after the tragedy including installing hatches that could be opened from the outside, removing flammable material from the CM, and using a nitrogen-oxygen mixture for the atmosphere in the CM.

---

22. Williams, 2011.
23. Williams, 2011.

UNMANNED APOLLO MISSIONS

After the tragedy of *Apollo 1*, NASA had to regroup and make changes to the program. After that fateful day in January, NASA launched three unmanned missions starting with Apollo 4 (there was no *Apollo 2* or *3*) before sending men into space once more.

Apollo 4 launched November 9, 1967

Apollo 5 launched January 22, 1968

Apollo 6 launched April 4, 1968

Apollo 7

Time was running out. If NASA wanted to beat President Kennedy's clock, they would have to resume manned flights. On October 10, 1968, Walter "Wally" Schirria, Walter "Walt" Cunningham, and Donn Eisele became the first crew of the Apollo program to complete a manned mission into space. The 11-day quest was a success, with the only problem being that the crew experienced severe head colds during the mission. During *Apollo 7*'s mission, they sent seven television transmissions back to Earth — the first live broadcasts from a manned U.S. spacecraft.

Apollo 8

Frank Borman, James A. Lovell, and William A. Anders made up the crew of *Apollo 8*. Their mission was the first in the Apollo program to orbit the Moon. The spacecraft launched December 21, 1968, successfully returning on December 27. Six live transmissions took place, including a Christmas Eve broadcast in which the astronauts read from the book of Genesis.

Apollo 9

On March 3, 1969, NASA launched *Apollo 9* with just over a year left in the alloted decade. The previous Apollo missions had been successful, but could scientists really land a man on the Moon? James McDivitt, David Scott, and Russell Schweickart prepared to do their part to make that dream a reality for the American people. Launching on March 3, 1969, the crew of *Apollo 9* tested the new spacesuits and the LM in Earth's orbit. This was a crucial mission necessary before NASA could attempt to send man to the Moon. Ten days later, the mission was complete and the astronauts returned safely to Earth.

Apollo 10

Thomas P. Stafford, John W. Young, and Eugene A. Cernan's — the crew of *Apollo 10* — mission was a sort of dress rehearsal for a lunar landing. On May 18, 1969, the astronauts became the second crew to orbit the Moon. Their mission was the first to launch with all three components of the spacecraft. The crew did everything *Apollo 11* would do, except make a n actual lunar landing. The astronauts returned to Earth without incident on May 26.

SPACESUITS

Obviously, NASA couldn't send men to walk on the Moon without proper protective gear. The Moon's atmosphere is different than Earth's, so to keep the astronauts safe, NASA had to create portable environments in the form of spacesuits.

Here's a look at what you might encounter if you landed on the Moon, squeezed out of the capsule, and trotted off without the protection of a space suit:

- There's no oxygen. Without it, your brain would get all fuzzy and you would feel dizzy. Then *plop,* you would lose consciousness within a minute or two.

- The Sun feels **HOT** from the Moon's surface; we're talking *250-degree-Fahrenheit hot.* At this extreme temperature, your skin could very well melt right off.

- While in the light, it's hotter than hot, it's **COLD** in the murky shadows. "I love winter," you might say. Well, you've never experienced the intense coldness of a minus 250-degree Moon. Without protection, your fingers might *snap* off from the cold.

As you can see, spacesuits are an absolute necessity. But remember, this was unfamiliar territory. Scientists didn't know what to expect from the Moon's atmosphere. It took years of trial and error to perfect the spacesuits for the NASA astronauts. It also took a lot of people to test the suits, including designers, engineers, spacesuit testers — and of course, the astronauts.

Various types of spacesuits.

─────── *FAST FACT* ───────────────────

The *Apollo 11* crew had three custom-made spacesuits each. One suit was for training, while the other two were for the mission.

The spacesuits for *Apollo 11* evolved from the early ones made for Project Mercury. Remember, during these missions, the astronauts didn't actually leave the spacecraft. When man began spacewalks during the Gemini missions, the suits were fitted with life-sustaining oxygen hoses connected to the spacecraft.

The next stage of evoliving the suits involved creating systems that could support the astronauts' lunar walk. The portable life support system allowed the men to venture from the spacecraft onto the lifeless terrain of the Moon. To do this, they also needed specially designed lunar boots.

─────── *FAST FACT* ───────────────────

NASA contracted with ILC Dover to create the Apollo spacesuits and lunar boots. The Delaware-based company continues to work with NASA today.

The early Apollo missions proved that humans could probably survive a lunar trip. Scientists at NASA now needed one final piece to complete the puzzle of a lunar landing: three men to make the journey.

Chapter 3

THE ASTRONAUTS OF APOLLO 11

AFTER THE SUCCESS OF THE EARLY APOLLO MISSIONS, IT was time to get down to business. The end of the decade was approaching. Would NASA meet the president's deadline? Deke Slayton had a crucial decision to make. Which crew would man the lunar mission and, most importantly, which astronaut would take the most crucial first step in history?

THE *APOLLO 11* ASTRONAUTS: SELECTION

In December 1968, Deke Slayton had exciting news for Neil Armstrong. If *Apollo 8* returned safely from her mission *and* if things went smoothly for *Apollo 9* and *10*, Armstrong would command *Apollo 11*. The *Apollo 11* astronauts, hopefully, would make the first lunar landing.

Slayton decided that Armstrong was a strong candidate after the *Gemini 8* emergency. Accroding to Slayton, Armstrong's "... abilities to reason, to think, to handle emergencies, to fly ... anything from the Wright brothers' planes to rocket ships ..." had nudged his name to the top of the list. [24]

---

24. Barbree, 2014.

But Slayton kept his plans secret until *Apollo 8* was in orbit. When Slayton pulled Armstrong aside and told him he might command *Apollo 11*, his reply was priceless: "That wouldn't make me mad," Armstrong said. [25]

Ever humble, Armstrong thanked Slayton for having confidence in him to potentially command what would be the first lunar mission. "If you decide to trust me with *Apollo 11*, you'll get my best effort," he said. [26]

As they shook hands, Slayton said that he knew he could count on him. Armstrong felt honored but wasn't completely sure a lunar landing was in his immediate future. Too many things could go wrong with the next three planned missions.

Later, the two men discussed who would accompany Armstrong on the *Apollo 11* mission. "How would you feel about having Collins and Buzz Aldrin as your crew?" Slayton asked. [27] Armstrong said it wouldn't be a problem.

Months passed. The gossip around NASA was that Slayton was close to announcing his selection for the *Apollo 11* crew. On January 4, 1969, Slayton summoned Collins and Aldrin to his office where Armstrong was already waiting.

Slayton got straight to the point. Armstrong would command *Apollo 11*, Collins would handle the CM, and Aldrin would manage the LM and direct the experiments.

25. Barbree, 2014.
26. Barbree, 2014.
27. Barbree, 2014.

NASA made the crew announcement on January 9. They also announced that the astronauts were training for a potential Moon landing and that Armstrong would take that first step.

NAMING SPACECRAFTS

NASA had previously prohibited the astronauts from naming their spacecraft, but with *Apollo 9*, they changed their minds. Here are the names of the Apollo modules:

Apollo 9: CM - Gumdrop; LM - Spider

Apollo 10: CM - Charlie Brown; LM - Snoopy

Apollo 11: CM - Columbia; LM - Eagle

Apollo 12: CM - Yankee Clipper; LM - Intrepid

Apollo 13: CM - Odyssey; LM - Aquarius

Apollo 14: CM - Kitty Hawk; LM - Antares

Apollo 15: CM - Endeavor; LM - Falcon

Apollo 16: CM - Casper; LM - Orion

Apollo 17: CM - America; LM - Challenger

WHO WERE THE MEN OF *APOLLO 11*?

Before we learn about the mission, let's learn more about these space pioneers.

Neil Armstrong

Neil Armstrong's portrait for NASA.

The first man to walk on the Moon was born July 5, 1930 in Wapakoneta, Ohio. When Armstrong was six years old, his father took him on his first airplane ride, although Neil would later admit that he didn't recall the event. The plane was the Ford Tri-Motor, nicknamed the "Tin Goose" or "Flying Washboard" because of its all-metal body.

Neil's father, Stephen, was a state auditor. The family moved from county to county as Stephen Armstrong poured through financial records looking for red flags. His mother, Viola, was a stay-at-home mother like most women in the 1930s.

By the time Armstrong was 10 years old, he had lived in many Ohio cities including Cleveland, Warren, Jefferson, St. Marys, and Upper Sandusky. As a young boy, Armstrong loved building model airplanes. Although Stephen Armstrong earned a decent living, he required his three children earn money to pay for their own hobbies.

Armstrong earned money to buy his model kits by cutting grass at a local cemetery. Then he found a job working at a bakery cleaning the mixing vats for 40¢ an hour.

Armstrong loved music and used some of his bakery money to buy a baritone horn. He joined his school's band and continued to play through college.

FAST FACT:

Armstrong was a charter member of a new Boy Scout Troop in which he earned the highest rank, Eagle Scout.

When Armstrong was in high school, his father got a new job working for the Department of Public Welfare. The family returned to Wapakoneta. In addition to the band, in high school Armstrong was active in the glee club and student council.

Armstrong's love of airplanes continued but now he had a different goal in mind: he wanted to fly. After saving the money he earned by working jobs around town, Armstrong took flying lessons.

FAST FACT

Armstrong's flying lessons cost $9 an hour. That's the equivalent of about $120 per hour in 2018 currency.

Armstrong worked hard and got his pilot's license on his 16th birthday. He couldn't drive yet, but he could fly!

In the fall of 1947, Armstrong left for college. His parents couldn't afford college tuition and although he saved money from his jobs, it wasn't enough. However, the U.S. Naval Aviation College Program offered scholarships to students who agreed to serve three years in the Navy. The scholarships allowed students to attend any accredited four-year college.

Armstrong chose Purdue, located in West Lafayeet, Indiana, 150 miles away from home. Purdue was an excellent choice for Armstrong. The university had an outstanding aeronautical engineering program.

After three semesters, the Navy called Armstrong up to active duty. In 1949, he arrived in Pensacola, Florida for flight school. Armstrong's training got off to a bumpy start, but he soon became a skilled military pilot.

It wasn't long before Armstrong got the opportunity to demonstrate his skills. In 1950, after the Korean War began, Armstrong became a member of Fighter Squadron 51. The 20-year-old pilot was the youngest of the California-based jet squadron.

Assigned to the *USS Essex*, Armstrong mastered takeoffs and landings — a difficult skill that would prove useful years later when he became an astronaut. In June of 1950, Armstrong and the *USS Essex* headed to Korea.

Armstrong flew 78 missions during the Korean War, receiving several medals for his service. On August 23, 1952, he left the Navy with the rank of lieutenant, junior grade in the U.S. Naval Reserve.

Armstrong returned to college in the fall of 1952, leading an active social life. He joined the band, Aero Club, Phi Delta Theta Fraternity, and the American Rocket Society. At Purdue, Armstrong also met his future wife, Janet Shearon. Armstrong graduated in 1955 with a degree in aeronautical engineering.

After college, he landed a job at National Advisory Committee for Aeronautics (NACA) as a research pilot for Lewis Flight Propulsion Laboratory in Cleveland, Ohio.

———— FAST FACT ————

National Advisory Committee for Aeronautics (NACA) was the predecessor to NASA.

While this job launched his career, Armstrong was itching to work at the Edwards Air Force Base in California. The facility was involved in some exciting *boundary-pushing* experiments. His wish soon came true. Armstrong received a job offer, and he was off to California.

But first, he had to make a stop in Wisconsin. His girlfriend Janet was working a summer job at a camp there and Armstrong had decided to propose.

"You know," he began, "I've been thinking." [28]

"Oh," said Janet.

"If you would marry me and come with me in the car to Edwards, NACA would reimburse me six cents per mile instead of four," he joked.

"Sort of makes marriage worth considering, right?"

"Right. How about it?"

"Well ... Perhaps it's a thought that should be considered."

She didn't hop in the car and head to California with Armstrong, but they did marry a few months later, on January 28, 1956. The Armstrongs welcomed their first child — Eric Alan — on June 30, 1957. His parents nicknamed the new baby, Ricky. The couple had two more kids: Karen Ann (born April 13, 1959) — called Muffie — and Mark (born April 8, 1963).

---

28. Barbree, 2014.

After the Soviets victory with Sputnik, the newly-created NASA was on the hunt for astronauts. While many men answered the call, Armstrong wasn't one of them. He wasn't interested in being an astronaut at the moment. He was happy as a test pilot and he loved his work as an engineer. Armstrong was also a very private person. He didn't like the idea of the publicity that would follow inevitably this momentous project.

Armstrong continued to test new airplanes, including the X-15 "rocket plane." Armstrong would eventually take the experimental plane upwards to an altitude over 200,000 feet and soar at speeds exceeding 4,000 miles an hour.

FAMILY TRAGEDY

Armstrong experienced a tragedy no parent should: the death of a child. In 1961, his daughter Karen tripped and bumped her head while on a trip to Seattle, Washington. Everything seemed fine until the Armstrongs noticed that Karen was having trouble with her vision. They took her to a local doctor who said she was fine, but suggested they take her to see her own doctor when they returned home.

Back at home the news wasn't good. Karen had an inoperable brain tumor. After a round of radiation treatment, she went into remission but it was short-lived. The 3-year-old died on January 28, 1962 — her parents' wedding anniversary.

In April 1962, NASA announced they needed more astronaut candidates. Over 250 applied, and this time, Neil Armstrong was among the applicants. As we read earlier, Armstrong joined eight other men and become the "New Nine," the second group of astronauts. These astronauts would complete the Gemini projects.

―――― *FAST FACT* ――――――――――――――――

Why did NASA choose "Gemini" as the name for the new project? It was a nod to the zodiac sign of the twins because each mission would carry two men.

―――――――――――――――――――――――――――――――

Armstrong's first assignment was to support the *Gemini 5*. He would train as commander and Elliot See would train as backup pilot. The Armstrong-See team would backup Gordon Cooper and Pete Conrad, stepping in if one or both astronauts were unable to make their flight.

First Trip in Space

Armstrong would get his chance to voyage beyond Earth's atmosphere as commander of *Gemini 8*. His partner was David Scott from the third group of astronauts. Their mission was to perfect the docking technique in space. During the mission, an astronaut would venture outside the spacecraft; NASA called this EVA or Extra-vehicular activity. Scott would complete the spacewalk.

On March 16, 1966, the *Gemini 8* spacecraft successfully launched. The two-man crew had to catch up with an unmanned spacecraft named *Agena* so that *Gemini 8* could test the docking scenario.

Three orbits later (4 hours and 48 minutes into their mission), Armstrong spotted what he thought could be the *Agena*. He radioed Mission Control with the news, adding, "It could be a planet." [29]

―――――――――

29. Barbree, 2014.

Armstrong was eventually able to verify that it was indeed the Agena. Soon, the two spacecrafts — one unmanned, one with two passengers — raced around the Earth together at speeds of over 17,000 miles per hour.

Because of Armstrong's time in the simulators, he successfully docked with the *Agena*. Back at Mission Control, everyone was ecstatic. Deke Slayton passed out cigars like he was a new dad. The docking took place about six and a half hours into the mission.

FAST FACT

Before the actual docking, the team orbited in unison with the *Agena* for several hours. NASA called this "station-keeping."

But they weren't out of the woods yet. For 21 minutes the crew wouldn't be able to communicate with Mission Control as they orbited over the Indian Ocean. This communication pause — LOS (loss of signal) — is like a dead zone where you can't get cell phone reception.

After 21 minutes of radio silence, the first thing Mission Control heard was Scott's frantic voice. Scott reported they were tumbling and had disengaged from the Agena. While docked, Scott noticed the two spacecrafts weren't level but had tilted. Armstrong tried to correct the problem but couldn't, so he decided to disengage.

They continued to tumble end-over-end. At this rate, the astronauts would lose consciousness soon. One of spacecraft's thrusters was stuck in the firing position, but there were 16 thrusters and Armstrong was already feeling woozy.

Armstrong realized they had one chance at survival — he would have to fire the Reentry Control System (RCS) thrusters. It worked and Armstrong was back in control of the *Gemini* capsule.

Unfortunately, they would have to abandon the remainder of the mission. NASA required astronauts to immediately return home if they activate the RCS thrusters. The mission was over, but the crew was safe.

FAST FACT

Colleagues often described Armstrong as somewhat aloof and distant. He was a man of few words and was immensely private. But most also agree he had an analytical mind and was extremely cool and calm under pressure. People who worked with Armstrong greatly admired him.

Edwin "Buzz" Aldrin, Jr.

Edwin "Buzz" Aldrin's portrait for NASA.

"The first time I applied to be an astronaut, NASA turned me down," [30] said Edwin "Buzz" Aldrin. Fortunately, Aldrin persevered, landing a spot in the third class. He would go down in history as the second man to walk on the Moon.

Born January 20, 1930 in Montclair, New Jersey, Aldrin was the son of a U.S. Air Force pilot. His mother Marion Moon (yes, his mom's maiden name was Moon, ironically) was the daughter of an Army chaplain.

---

30. Aldrin, 2016.

Aldrin's dad won an airplane in a contest and took young Buzz on his first plane ride when he was two. Ironically, the plane — christened the *Eagle* — shared the same name as *Apollo 11's* lunar module.

────── FAST FACT ──────────────────────

Where did the nickname "Buzz" come from? When he was younger, his sister, Fay Ann, couldn't say the word "brother," so instead, she called him "buzzer". The family shortened the nickname and he's been Buzz ever since. In 1988, he legally changed his name to Buzz.

Like Armstrong, Aldrin loved building model planes as a child and had a passion for aviation. As an adolescent he became fascinated with the inner workings of airplanes. He wanted to know how they functioned and how they could operate better.

After graduating high school (one year early) in 1947, Aldrin enrolled in the United States Military Academy at West Point in New York. In 1951, he graduated third in his class, earning a B.S. in electrical engineering.

After college Aldrin joined the U. S. Air Force, where he trained as a fighter pilot. He was a member of the 51st Fighter Wing, flying 66 combat missions during the Korean War. Armstrong received a Distinguished Flying Cross for his service.

In 1953, Aldrin enrolled at the Massachusetts Institute of Technology (MIT). He planned to earn his master's degree and then go to flight school. He ended up staying at MIT to pursue his doctorate, which he earned in 1963.

Aldrin met his wife Joan Archer in the early 1950s while Aldrin was in the Air Force. They married in 1954 and had three children: James, Janice, and Andrew.

Although NASA at first denied him, Aldrin set his mind on becoming an astronaut, but he wasn't a test pilot. Aldrin dreamed of joining the space program after his friend, Ed White, signed on with NASA. "If space was going to be our next new frontier, I wanted to be part of getting there," Aldrin said. [31]

NASA accepted Aldrin into the third class of trainees. One of the reasons NASA had an interest in Aldrin was his ideas on rendezvous. Aldrin received a doctorate in astronautics from MIT. "For my thesis, I adapted my experience as a fighter pilot during the Korean War, where I had focused on intercepting enemy aircraft, and devised a technique for two manned spacecraft [sic] to meet in space, a procedure called manned orbital rendezvous," he said. [32]

FAST FACT

Over 6,000 applicants applied for the third class of NASA astronauts.

Spacewalk

Aldrin was the pilot for *Gemini 12*, where he set a world record for space-walking. He joked it was "... more of a space *float*, rather than a five and a half hours' "walk" in space ..." [33]

---

31. Aldrin, 2016.
32. Aldrin, 2016.
33. Aldrin, 2016.

During his "walk" Aldrin — fastened to the spacecraft by a long cord — circled Earth every 90 minutes, at a speed of 17,500 miles per hour.

Although a part of the astronaut training program, Aldrin wasn't originally a part of a flight crew for the Gemini missions. Instead, he pulled backup crew duty. The tragic deaths of Charlie Bassett and Elliot See propelled him higher on the assignment list, first as backup for *Gemini 9* and then as crew for *Gemini 12*.

Aldrin denies claims that he made a big stink about not being the first to walk on the Moon. According to NASA procedures, he should have been. Normally, the commander remains in the spacecraft, while the pilot performs the EVAs. That was the procedure prior to *Apollo 11*.

With the lunar landing, both the pilot and the commander would take Moonwalks. Because the event was historic, Deke Slayton decided the commander should emerge first. Reports cite seniority as another reason Armstrong took the first step.

——— *FAST FACT* ————————————

Although Armstrong was the first to step foot on the Moon, Aldrin says he was the first to "... relieve his bladder on the Moon." [34] He said: "When Neil took one small step for man and one giant leap for mankind; I took one small step and one giant *leak* for mankind!" [35]

Some of Aldrin's buddies said he should go first, but he said it didn't matter. He claims he would have even been content to pilot a later mission. Aldrin knew there would be a lot of publicity, and he didn't want it. He'd already experienced unwanted attention after the Gemini mission.

34. Aldrin, 2016.
35. Aldrin, 2016.

He was grateful for the kindness shown to him upon his return but sometimes it was overwhelming. "I could barely step outside our home without being swarmed by media or fans," he said. [36]

He believes it was also too much for his mother. "I'm convinced that the emotional overload following my Gemini success was a major factor in my mother committing suicide the year before I went to the Moon," he said.[37]

FAST FACT

Aldrin stepped on the Moon 19 minutes after Neil Armstrong.

Michael Collins

Michael Collins's portrait for NASA.

Like the two other *Apollo 11* astronauts, Michael Collins has his own place in history. Sometimes referred to as the forgotten astronaut, Collins would not get the opportunity to walk on the Moon like his colleagues.

Collins was born on Halloween Day 1930 in Rome, Italy. His father was stationed in Italy at the time of Collins' birth. James Collins was a U.S. Army Major General. He moved the family to Washington when the United States entered World War II.

Collins' dad was a military attaché, or diplomat. The family moved frequently when Collins was young. He lived in Oklahoma; Governors Island

---

36. Aldrin, 2016.
37. Aldrin, 2016.

(near New York City), New York; Baltimore; Columbus, Ohio; San Antonio; and San Juan, Puerto Rico — all before he was 10.

While living in Puerto Rico, Collins took his first plane ride. "The pilot even let me steer a little bit ..." Collins said. [38] But unlike Armstrong and Aldrin, Collins didn't have a passion for airplanes. Like many young men at the time, he dabbled in model airplane building, but he was more interested in chess, football, and girls.

After high school, Collins attended West Point, where he graduated in 1952 with a Bachelor of Science degree. He joined the U.S. Air Force after college, training as a pilot in Columbus, Mississippi.

Collins came from a family of Army men. His family assumed he would follow his dad, two uncles, his brother, and a cousin into the service. Collins decided to join the Air Force because he wanted to make it on his own without any familial influence.

Collins trained in Mississippi for six months, then moved to San Marcos and Waco, Texas for additional training. He got his wings in 1953 and was selected for advanced fighter training at Nellis Air Force Base in Las Vegas, Nevada.

Collins thought he was going to Korea. Instead, he was deployed to California. He was a member of the 21st Fighter Bomber Wing where he trained in ground attacks and how to deliver nuclear weapons.

In 1954, his unit relocated to France, then West Germany in 1956. After the war, Collins was an experimental test pilot at the Edwards Air Force Base in California.

---

38. Collins, 1974.

Collins married Patricia Finnegan in 1957. Before the couple could say, "I do," Collins had to overcome one problem. Finnegan's came from a family of devout Catholic, but Collins was Episcopalian. Before accepting his proposal, Finnegan told Collins he needed to get permission from her father. Fortunately, he was persuasive and Mr. Finnegan gave Collins the green light.

The couple had three children: Kathleen (Kate), born May 6, 1959; Ann, born October 31, 1961 (same day as her dad); and Michael, born February 23, 1963.

FAST FACT

Kate Collins is an actress best known for her role on the daytime soap opera, *All My Children.*

When Collins saw John Glenn command Mercury's *Atlas 6,* he knew he wanted to be an astronaut. He applied during the second call-out. Like Aldrin, NASA rejected Collins' first application.

He then enrolled in the U.S. Air Force Aerospace Research Pilot School. When NASA put out a call for astronauts the third time, Collins applied. NASA accepted him and in 1963, he joined the third cluster of astronauts.

FAST FACT

Collins was part of the backup crew for the *Gemini 7* mission.

Gemini 10 spacewalk

Collins' first space mission was on July 18, 1966. Collins and John Young's *Gemini 10* mission achieved the first double space rendezvous. During the mission, Collins took two spacewalks. But that wasn't all. Collins said, after he had a chance to review the EVA objectives, he realized the enormity of the mission. In addition to the spacewalks and rendezvous, there were 15 experiments.

During the three-day mission, the men successfully completed their objectives. They were so focused and quiet that Slayton had to radio the men to talk more so that Mission Control would have a better idea of what was going on.

FAST FACT

Collins was supposed to have flown with the *Apollo 8* crew, but he was recuperating from back surgery.

APOLLO 11 ASTRONAUT TRAINING

Much of the training for the Apollo 11 crew took place in simulators — exact replicas of the command and lunar modules. The models were complete with switches and warning lights. The controls, linked to a computer program, tested the astronauts' response to normal and emergency situations.

To give astronauts the feel for what they would encounter during their missions, movie and television displays surrounded the "spacecraft." The astronauts saw the Earth, Moon, stars, and even other spacecraft docking.

Other training devices included:

The Lunar Landing Training Vehicle (LLTV)

The LLTV trained astronauts to pilot the lunar module. Armstrong had an issue with his vehicle on May 5, 1968 when during a training exercise, he noticed he was losing control of the LLTV. If he didn't act fast, he would crash. He made a smart decision: he hit the "eject" button. The vehicle plummeted to the ground and burst into flames. Luckily, Armstrong's ejection seat catapulted him high above flames and he parachuted away from the burning wreckage.

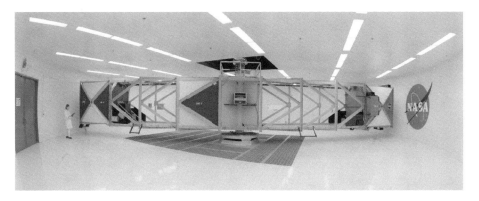

The Lunar Landing Training Vehicle (LLTV).

The Wheel

Astronauts trained on a centrifuge device known as "the wheel." The machine had a long steel arm with a capsule at the end (made to look like the cockpit). The trainees practiced what it was like to reenter Earth from space. Doctors monitored their vitals on close-circuit TV during the testing. A camera caught the tortured astronaut's face as the scientists tested on the effects of acceleration and deceleration on the human body.

A centrifuge used during NASA training.

FAST FACT

How many hours did the *Apollo 11* crew spend training in simulators? The men estimated that they spent 2,000 hours from the announcement in January to their launch in July 1969.

The astronauts learned:

- How to use pressure suits, ejection seats, and parachutes

- How to free float

- How to eat and drink in weightlessness

- Water safety and survival skills

- Lessons in camera usage

- Astronomy

The men also spent time in the gym and doing other physical activities like jogging or playing tennis.

The trainings were dress rehearsals. When Armstrong and Aldrin practiced their lunar mission, they were in full gear, including the white spacesuits, complete with gear-filled backpacks. The gear on Earth weighed 200 pounds, so you can imagine how difficult it was to walk.

In space, the gear would only weigh about one-sixth of that, or 33 pounds. The *Apollo 11* crew trained every day for six months to prepare for the lunar trip. They jetted from NASA's Houston base to Kennedy (Florida) and Edwards (California). The men participated in numerous press conferences and public appearances.

According to Armstrong, a third of their times was spent "... planning, figuring out techniques and methods that would allow us to achieve the trajectories and the sequence of events and the ways of picking from the available strategies the one that might work best." [39]

The last third was testing — thousands of hours in the labs, spacecrafts, etc. — and familiarizing themselves with the various systems. Armstrong pointed out that training was different; since no one had done it before, there was no one to tell them *how* to the do it.

Deke Slayton agreed: "We didn't know how to train an astronaut in those days. We would use any training device or method that had even a remote

---

39. Nelson, 2009.

chance of being useful, and we would make the training as difficult as possible so that we would be overtrained rather than undertrained." [40]

Aldrin and Armstrong did most of their training together. Collins often trained alone on machines like the docking simulator in Langley, Virginia. Then the men would fly to Delaware to test the spacesuits. It was a whirlwind time and the astronauts typically worked 14-hour days. They often didn't make it home.

FAST FACT

The astronauts were so busy training and making appearances, they had use of their own two-seater T-38 planes to fly to meetings or training locations. Of course, they also used the planes to fly home and spend a limited amount of time with their families.

In the years following President Kennedy's challenge, NASA worked diligently to beat the clock. They successfully found and trained astronauts, and unmanned and manned missions experienced both triumph and loss. With the Mercury, Gemini, and early Apollo missions complete, it was now time for a lunar mission.

---

40. Nelson, 2009.

Chapter 4

BUILDING AND DESIGNING THE *APOLLO 11* SPACECRAFT

WE READ IN CHAPTER 2 THAT THE *APOLLO 11* SPACECRAFT was comprised of three separate components: the Command Module (CM) *Columbia*; the Service Module (SM); and *Eagle*, the Lunar Module (LM). This chapter explores the building and design of these crucial units. Although each component had a separate function, when combined, the trio worked in harmony to assure a successful lunar landing.

Astronauts and NASA personnel often referred to the Command Module and Service Module as one unit — the Command-Service Module, or CSM. The Apollo spacecraft provided more than transportation. The segments offered protection from the harsh elements, a place to sleep and work, and fuel supply for the return trip.

Two essential components supported the CSM and LM. The Spacecraft Lunar Module Adapter (SLA) shielded the LM from the stress of liftoff and connected the CSM to the Saturn launcher. Close your eyes and picture a cone with the tip missing — that's what the SLA looked like.

The SLA was 28 feet long. The diameter at the base was 260 inches, narrowing to 154 inches at the Service Module mating line. The SLA weighed 4,009 pounds. The Launch Escape System (LES) sat on top of this protective shield.

The LES was a key component. In an emergency, the LES could whisk the crew away from the launch vehicle in the CM to safety. The top of the structure was cone-shaped. The body was a slender rocket stacked on top of another structure resembling a signal tower. The structure had an open frame. The LES was mounted to the CM by four bolts. The system had three propellant rockets, ready to blast the crew to safety in an emergency. The LES was 33 feet tall with a 4-foot diameter and weighed a hefty 8,910 pounds.

Both components dropped away once the spacecraft was on the right trajectory, leaving only the Command, Service, and Lunar Modules. Let's look closer at the three modules.

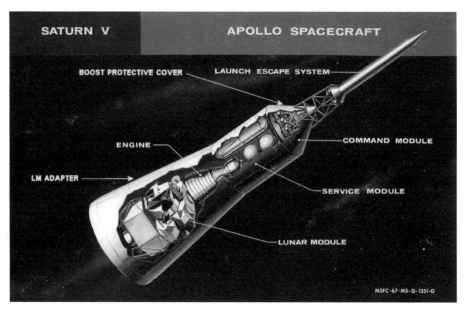

A diagram of the Apollo 11 spacecraft.

THE COMMAND MODULE *COLUMBIA*

As stated previously, the Command Module is the only part of the spacecraft to return to Earth. North American Rockwell, a NASA aerospace contractor company, built the CM for the *Apollo 11* mission. Command Module 107 was about the size of the interior of a large car. It served as the crew's living quarters, so obvioulsy, the tiny enclosure was *not* for the claustrophobic. The cone-shaped capsule was 10 feet, 7 inches tall, its diameter was 12 feet, 10 inches, and it weighed a whopping 13,000 pounds at launch (including the crew).

The CM was enclosed in a heat shield three layers deep to protect its precious cargo. The tip of the module contained the hatch and docking assembly for rendezvous with the LM. Like a human fetus is connected to its mother through the umbilical cord — the CM connected to the SM with an umbilical connector bearing the same name. The connector allowed water, coolant, and electrical power to pass between the two modules.

North American Rockwell employed 14,000 people to work on this segment, and 8,000 companies helped in the effort. The company, now known as Rockwell International, also built the Service Module.

The Command Module was separated into three parts:

1. The parachutes rested in the nose of the cone. A forward heat shield protected the parachutes and other sensitive equipment during re-entry. Once the spacecraft landed safely on Earth, the shield was jettisoned (was discarded).

2. Near the base of the CM, a compartment housed the propellant tanks, reaction control engines, wiring, and plumbing.

3. The largest part was the crew's living space, which was only about 218 cubic feet.

FAST FACT ————————————————————

The Command Module had:

- *2 million individual parts*
- *15 miles of wire*
- *a 24-instrument control panel*
- *566 switches*
- *40 indicators*
- *71 lights*

How did the crew access the CM? To enter and exit the crew cabin, astronauts used the main entrance on the side of the module. A second entrance on the forward docking tunnel allowed the astronauts to enter and leave the module during lunar docking.

Inside the Crew Quarters

The compact quarters used every inch of available space. Inside the CM were three forward-facing seats or couches that sat side-by-side in the middle of the compartment. The couches were specially molded for each astronaut.

An access tunnel led the way to the docking hatch. The space is bursting with controls, displays, and all necessary navigation instruments.

The crew could peek out of five windows:

(1) located in the access hatch

(2) next to each astronaut in the two outer seats, and

(3) forward-facing rendezvous windows.

The Apollo 11 crew inside the Command Module.

FAST FACT

Just in case the astronauts had to make a few minor patch-ups, the CM contained a repair kit. The Velcro pouch had several tools including wrenches, screws, and handles.

We know the couches were specially molded, but how were they arranged? Collins occupied the right seat. Aldrin sat in the middle. Armstrong sat in the left seat. Armstrong's position was closest to the abort handle. If an emergency arose during launch, the commander could abort or end the mission. To do so, he would take the following steps:

1. Armstrong would turn the handle 30 degrees counterclockwise;

2. Three rockets — located above the crew — would fire;

3. The Command Module would yank free from the Service Module and everything below it.

The couches — suspended on a joint frame — moved independently of the other structures. This design created a cushion to soften the impact of an emergency landing on a solid surface. Each astronaut could individually adjust his couch, from flat to an 85-degree seated position. The couches had individual head rests and foot supports.

When the crew needed more workspace, they removed the center couch. After placing it under the left seat, the men could stand and work.

In the crew quarters, the voyagers are squeezed together elbow-to-elbow in their bulky white suits. What else would we find if we peeked inside the CM?

- Under the couches, were the sleeping quarters within a crawl space. The astronauts snoozed in enclosed hammocks. There were also lockers for food, clothes, and auxiliary or support equipment.

- The right side of the equipment bay was the area for urination only. The men deficated in a plastic bag wherever they floated.

The left side of the compartment was for storing and preparing food.

- How do you keep objects from floating around in an environment without gravity? Why, Velcro, of course! Velcro has two distinct sides. The fluffy side is the eye (or female) and the coarse side is the hook (or male). The walls contained squares of the Velcro hooks. The instruments had squares of the eye side glued on. When the astronauts needed to place an object down temporarily, he affixed the eye to the hook.

The CM was designed as a three-man operation during launch, while in orbit, and when transferring to and from the LM. During the lunar mission, one astronaut has the task of controlling the ship.

The Command Module's console takes up most of the cramped space. It's almost 7-feet long and extends three feet upward.

In front of each seat are controls. The astronauts perform the task associated with the controls in front of him. As mentioned earlier, the crew typically sits in a particular order, however, during some tasks, they may switch seats. The center position is mainly concerned with navigation. The left seat handles flight-control and the right couch tackles the ship's subsystems.

FAST FACT

The types of controls or switches found on the consoles are usually toggle (most commonly used), pushbutton, or rotary.

THE SERVICE MODULE

It seems like the Command and Lunar Modules got all the attention because of their important roles in the historic mission. But the Service Module was equally significant. Service Module 107 attached to the CM. It was 24 feet, 7 inches tall and had a diameter of 12 feet, 10 inches. At launch, the SM weighed 51,243 pounds.

The Service Module — shaped like a cylinder — stored the main Service Propulsion System engine. The propulsion system is the rocket engine that launched the spacecraft into orbit and got it safely home. Six additional sections housed:

(3) 31-cell hydrogen-oxygen fuel cells

(2) cryogenic oxygen tanks

(2) cryogenic hydrogen tank

(4) tanks for the main propulsion engine — (2) fuel and (2) oxygen

(2) helium tanks

Subsystems for the main propulsion units.

Three tension ties connected the SM and CM, along with the umbilical connector mentioned before. We know the SM didn't return to Earth. So how did the crew get rid of it?

When it was time for reentry, the team switched the CM to internal battery power. After separating from the SM, two steel blades severed the connections between the two units. The CM returned safely to Earth, while the SM remained in space, eventually burning up in the atmosphere.

THE LUNAR MODULE *EAGLE*

The *Eagle* was 22 feet, 11 inches long and 31 feet wide. It weighed 8,650 pounds while empty, but with the crew and propellant, it weighed 32,500. Intended to only fly in space, engineers designed the LM differently than the other components. For example, it didn't have a heat shield to protect the craft during reentry because it remained on the Moon. The LM was originally called the Lunar Excursion Module (LEM). After the name change, many at NASA continued to call the module LEM. Grumman Aerospace Corporation (now Northrup Grumman) built the Lunar Module.

The LM was an odd-looking creature that "... resembled an awkward giant bug," said astronaut Jim McDivitt. [41] He also said it looked as delicate as tissue paper. It was the only major piece of hardware not tested by the *Apollo 11* astronauts. That honor went to the *Apollo 9* and *10* crews.

There were no seats on the LM. During the lunar mission, the two astronauts stood in the cockpit. Standing in front of two triangular windows, they had a good view of their surroundings. They could easily control their craft during descent to the lunar surface, and later, during ascent from the Moon.

Lunar Module 5 was a two-stage vehicle. The upper portion of the spacecraft was the ascent stage. The lower section was the descent stage. The capsule worked as a unit until the staging phase of the mission. This is when the ascent stage became a single spacecraft for CSM rendezvous and docking.

---

41. Shepard, 1994.

The descent stage was an octagonal-shaped vehicle, measuring 4.2 meters across and 1.7 meters thick. It had four legs with round footpads that prohibited the module from touching the lunar surface.

You have undoubtedly seen video of Armstrong's disembarkment from the Lunar Module. The platform and ladder he descends from is on one of the descent's legs. The descent stage also contained:

- the landing rocket

- (2) fuel tanks fuel

- (2) tanks nitrogen tetroxide oxidizer

- water

- oxygen and helium tanks

- storage space for the lunar equipment and experiments.

The irregularly shaped ascent stage was 2.8 meters tall and 4.0 by 4.3 meters wide. It mounted on top of the descent stage. The vehicle sheltered the crew and was the base of operation during the lunar experiments and maneuvers. Aldrin and Armstrong had 6.65 cubic feet of space in the ascent stage of the LM.

The lunar module had two hatches. One hatch allowed the astronauts to enter and exit the vehicle, while the other hatch on top was used for docking with the CSM. This section also contained a fuel and oxidizer tank; and helium, liquid oxygen, gaseous oxygen, and reactor control fuel tanks.

———— *FAST FACT* ————————————————————

The LM carried the Early Apollo Scientific Experiment Package (EASEP) — self-contained experiments, deployed and then left on the Moon. The EASEP contained additional scientific and sample collection kit.

The ascent stage of the LM was programmed to crash into the Moon after docking with the CM. NASA officials aren't sure exactly when it crashed. They estimate it crashed one to four months after the mission.

THE SATURN V ROCKET LAUNCHER

To propel the astronauts to the Moon, NASA needed a powerful rocket launcher. They chose the Saturn V. The 281-foot-high launcher was developed by NASA's Marshall Space Flight Center in Huntsville, Alabama. The rocket was field-tested on five previous occasions. It propelled two unmanned spacecrafts into orbit in 1967 and 1968. The Saturn V then blasted Apollo *8, 9,* and *10* crews into orbit. The Saturn V was one of the largest and most powerful launch rockets ever built.

The chief architect of the Saturn launcher was Dr. Wernher von Braun. Born in 1912 in Germany, von Braun developed an interest in space exploration at a young age. He began developing liquid-fuel rockets for the German army in 1932. In 1934, he earned a doctorate in physics, based on his research, which was funded by the German army.

Dr. von Braun and his team of rocket scientists developed the V-2 ballistic missile. The rocket was the precursor to the U.S. and Soviet intercontinental ballistic missiles and space launch vehicles.

As World War II was winding down, von Braun realized the Allies would probably capture Germany. In late 1944, he surrendered to the American forces, along with other key members of his team.

After the end of the war, von Braun developed ballistic missiles for the U.S. Army. In 1950, his team began working at the Redstone Arsenal in Huntsville, Alabama. They designed many missiles including the Redstone, Jupiter C, and Saturn I. It was Jupiter C that orbited with the first U.S. satellite, Explorer I.

In 1960, the task of rocket development was transferred from the U.S. Army to NASA. The main objective was to design powerful Saturn rockets. Dr. von Braun was named director of NASA's Marshall Space Flight Center. In addition to the Saturn V, von Braun's team designed the Redstone-Mercury rocket that propelled Shepard into suborbital flight.

Dr. von Braun moved to Washington, D.C. in 1970 to become head of a strategic planning committee. He retired from NASA in 1972 to take position at Fairchild Industries in Germantown, Maryland. Dr. von Braun died June 16, 1977.

Lunar Mission Staging

For the lunar mission, the Saturn V launched in three stages:

Stage 1 (S-IC): Saturn fires for 2.5 minutes. Apollo reaches speeds of 6,000 miles per hour. 37 miles into the sky, Stage 1 falls off into the ocean.

Stage 1 Specifications:

- Diameter: 33 feet

- Height: 138 feet

- 5,022,674 pounds (fueled)

- 288,750 pounds (dry)

- Engines: (5) F-1

- Propellants: Liquid oxygen & kerosene

Stage 2 (S-II): The launcher fires for 6 minutes. Apollo reaches speeds of 15,500 miles per hour. Stage 2 is dropped at 112 miles.

Stage 2 Specifications:

- Diameter: 33 feet

- Height: 81.5 feet

- 1,059,171 pounds (fueled)

- 79,918 pounds (dry)

- Engines: (5) J-2

- Propellants: Liquid oxygen & liquid hydrogen

Stage 3 (S-IVB): Saturn fires for 2 minutes, reaching a speed of 17,400 mph. The launcher remains with the crew until it's time to send them to the Moon. Saturn then fires for 5 minutes, sending the crew toward the Moon at 25,000 mph.

Stage 3 Specifications:

- Diameter: 21.7 feet

- Height: 58.3 feet

- 260,523 pounds (fueled)

- 25,000 pounds (dry)

- Engines: (1) J-2

- Propellants: Liquid oxygen & liquid oxygen

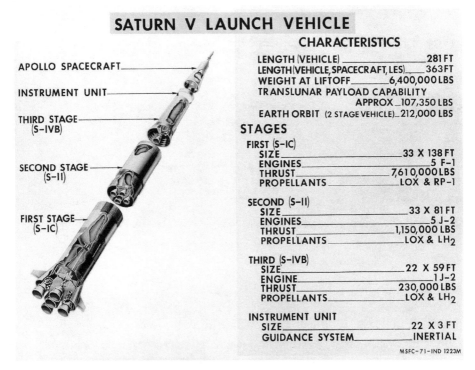

SATURN V LAUNCH VEHICLE
CHARACTERISTICS

APOLLO SPACECRAFT

INSTRUMENT UNIT

THIRD STAGE (S-IVB)

SECOND STAGE (S-II)

FIRST STAGE (S-IC)

LENGTH (VEHICLE)	281 FT
LENGTH (VEHICLE, SPACECRAFT, LES)	363 FT
WEIGHT AT LIFTOFF	6,400,000 LBS
TRANSLUNAR PAYLOAD CAPABILITY	APPROX 107,350 LBS
EARTH ORBIT (2 STAGE VEHICLE)	212,000 LBS

STAGES

FIRST (S-IC)
SIZE	33 X 138 FT
ENGINES	5 F-1
THRUST	7,610,000 LBS
PROPELLANTS	LOX & RP-1

SECOND (S-II)
SIZE	33 X 81 FT
ENGINES	5 J-2
THRUST	1,150,000 LBS
PROPELLANTS	LOX & LH_2

THIRD (S-IVB)
SIZE	22 X 59 FT
ENGINE	1 J-2
THRUST	230,000 LBS
PROPELLANTS	LOX & LH_2

INSTRUMENT UNIT
SIZE	22 X 3 FT
GUIDANCE SYSTEM	INERTIAL

MSFC-71-IND 1223M

A diagram of the Saturn V with its three stages.

Well-trained astronauts and capable rockets are only a part of what it takes to send a man to the Moon. For the third and final piece of the puzzle, we turn to the team at NASA — Mission Control.

Chapter 5

MISSION CONTROL

400,000 PEOPLE WERE RESPONSIBLE FOR THE LUNAR LAND-
ing, including:

> *Flight Directors . . .Flight Controllers . . . Flight Officers . . . Planners . . . Engineers . . . Rocket Designers . . . Technicians . . . Managers . . . Supervisors . . . Ground Controllers . . . Support Staff . . . Inspectors . . . Computer Programmers . . . Electricians . . . Welders . . . Seamstresses . . . Painters . . . Doctors . . . Geologists . . . Scientists . . . Pilots . . . Mathematicians . . . Radio Operators . . . Teletypists . . . Safety (SCUBA) Divers . . . Trainers . . . Navigators . . .*

The list goes on and on. Many of these positions operate behind the scenes. Their faces are rarely — if ever — seen. Mission Control is the visible team. These are the people we see in the control rooms, eyes glued to monitors. This chapter highlights a few of the essential Mission Control positions.

MISSION CONTROL CENTER

Mission Control Center (MCC) in Houston, Texas opened in 1965 with the *Gemini 4* operation. Previously the brain of the space program was operated from the Launch Control Center (LCC) at the Kennedy Space Center on Merritt Island, Florida.

The hub of activity was in the firing rooms, filled with hundreds of flight control engineers. In the firing room the launch director gives the final say on whether they mission is a "Go" or "No Go." He does not make the "Go" decision nonchalantly. He does so *only* after checking with key LCC pre-launch team members. Flight controllers perform crucial safety checks. Once they give the thumbs up, the launch director gives the "Go for launch" signal. The safety of the crew is the number one priority at all times.

The central control center is located three miles from the launch pad, but the controllers have a full view of the launch pad through huge heat and shock resistant double-paned windows. These windows extend the full width of the east wall of the firing rooms. The building has four floors, with the firing rooms located on the third level.

FAST FACT:

In January 2000, the Launch Control Center was placed on the *National Register of Historic Places*.

The firing room was arranged with raised platforms at the front, lowering to a set of cabinets shaped like a horseshoe. On the raised section the launch director and other important personnel, like test controllers, sat. The engineers occupied the lower levels. The LCC also had management rooms located off to the side. This allowed upper management to observe, but not interfere, with the controllers.

It was understood that once controllers entered the LCC on launch day, there was no joking around; this was serious business. Controllers had to focus on their responsibilities and their particular system.

The LCC staff was responsible for the final check of the launch vehicles. Once the vehicles were cleared for launch, the LCC team remained accountable until the spacecraft cleared the launch tower. Then the reins of the operation were turned over to Mission Control.

The Mission Control Center is housed in The Lyndon B. Johnson Space Center (JSC). The JSC, previously the Manned Spaceflight Center (1963-73), was renamed to honor the 36th U.S. president. During missions, astronauts use the radio call sign "Houston" when communicating with the MCC. A call sign is a shorthand naming system, typically used by pilots, law enforcement, and "ham" (amateur) radio enthusiasts.

The NASA Mission Control Center during Apollo 11.

Mission Control Center employees spend a small portion of their time "controlling missions" — only 10 percent, according to NASA. Here's how they divide the remainder of their working hours:

- 75 percent planning and organizing the mission

- 15 percent to their training and education

Like the LCC staff, the MCC team understands how important their jobs are. What are some assets of a MCC team member? *The Foundations of Mission Control* spells it out in black and white. There are five qualities essential for success:

Discipline: *Having the ability to follow as well as lead.*

Confidence: *Believing in yourself and others.*

Responsibility: *Being accountable for your work and not shifting your responsibilities (or the blame for not performing a task) to others.*

Toughness: *Being willing to keep trying, even if it means going in a different direction.*

Teamwork: *Working together to reach a common goal, realizing success depends on working cooperatively.*

Because MCC literally hold the lives of astronauts in their hands, their mission statement reminds employs:

"To always be aware that suddenly and unexpectedly we may find ourselves in a role where our performance has ultimate consequences." [42]

Mission Control includes two divisions: flight-control and ground-team workers.

---

42. Kranz, 2000.

The ground-team workers gather and analyze data, then decide how to proceed with each launch. The data comes from the spacecraft, launch facilities, and the flight control team. The information is used to develop response procedures. Some of the rules are generic and others are specific for each mission. Because each mission is different, the procedures are often modified for specific situations that surface.

While preparing for missions, astronauts train with MCC staff. It's impossible to plan for *every* situation, but the MCC trainers will run through typical scenarios. Sometimes the trainers are also tested. MCC workers may experience an anomaly. These built-in surprise glitches — called "sim-faults" — test the staff's ability to react quickly and respond logically.

The problem could be a simple equipment malfunction or a full-blown disaster. These exercises help Mission Control determine how prepared the ground crew are if a real emergency (minor or major) occurs.

The flight-control crew is what we think of as "mission control". During flights, the MOCR — Mission Operations Control Room (pronounced MOH-ker) — buzzes with excitement. Each flight controller's eyeballs are glued to their screens as data dances across the terminal.

FAST FACT

For today's shuttle missions, the MOCR was renamed the Flight Control Room.

It's impossible to discuss all the important positions in the MCC. That information could fill a separate book. There are some positions that are integral to the success of space missions. Let's look at a few.

Flight Director (FD or Flight)

The responsibility for the mission falls in the hands of the flight director. This includes managing the flight controllers and support staff. He is responsible for the payload which includes the crew and the cargo aboard the spacecraft. The FD's main consideration is protecting the mission crew.

Apollo 11 had three flight directors, responsible for various aspects of the mission:

- Gerald Griffin handled the launch and EVA

- Eugene Kranz had the momentous task of directing the lunar landing

- Glynn Lunney directed the lunar ascent

EUGENE "GENE" KRANZ

Kranz is probably the most well known of the three *Apollo 11* flight directors. Kranz was born in Toledo, Ohio in 1933. He had an interest in space travel from an early age. For a high school report, he even wrote about the possibility of a single-stage rocket trip to the Moon.

Kranz graduated from Parks College of St. Louis, Missouri, with a B.S. in Aeronautical Engineering. After college, he joined the U.S. Air Force, eventually serving in South Korea.

Kranz tested missile launchers for McDonnell Aircraft at Holloman Air Force Base in New Mexico. In 1960, he replied to a NASA employment ad in *Aviation Week*. Kranz was hired and began working as part of the Space Task Group at Langley Research Center in Hampton, Virginia.

Kranz worked in the Flight Control Operations Branch (1960-64). One of his duties was developing and writing rules used by flight directors. Kranz transferred to Houston when the Manned Space Center opened. His position was chief of Flight Control Operations. In addition to being the flight director for the *Apollo 11* lunar mission, Kranz guided the Gemini missions. He was instrumental in the safe return of the *Apollo 13* crew, which experienced an emergency during their mission.

Kranz had a long career with NASA. He served as flight operations director (1969-1974); deputy director of Flight Operations (1974-1983); and director of Mission Operations (1983-1994). Kranz retired from NASA in 1994.

Eugene "Gene" Kranz, one of the flight directors of Apollo 11.

Spacecraft Communicator (CapCom)

To avoid having too many people chatting with the mission crew, one person serves as the link between the astronauts and mission control. The Spacecraft Communicator or CapCom console was that link. The acronym was created during the time when spacecrafts were routinely called "capsules," so the Communicator would be talking to the capsules; hence CapCom. The name stuck.

Another astronaut is always the one to man the CapCom console on the ground. NASA believes only another astronaut can clearly communicate with the crew.

The men staffing the CapCom console were:

Landing CapCom — *Charles Duke*
Duke was part of the astronaut support backup crew for *Apollo 10* and backup LM pilot for *Apollo 13*. He was the LM pilot for the *Apollo 16* mission and backup LM pilot for *Apollo 17*.

Post-landing and Goodnight CapCom — *Owen Garriott*

EVA CapCom — *Bruce McCandless*
McCandless was part of the astronaut support backup crew for *Apollo 14*.

LM Launch CapCom — *Ronald Evans*
Evans served as astronaut support backup for *Apollo 7* and was backup CM pilot for *Apollo 14*. He was also CM pilot for the *Apollo 17* mission.

Flight Dynamics Officer (FDO)

The Flight Dynamics Operator or FDO (pronounced "FIDO") has the important job of planning maneuvers and monitoring the spacecraft's trajectory. If any changes need to be made during orbit, it's the FDO's responsibility to make those adjustments.

Apollo 11 FIDO:

> **Jay Green:** *LM descent stage*
>
> **Phillip Shaffer:** *LM ascent stage*
>
> **Guidance Officer (GUIDO)**

The GUIDO (pronounced "Guide-Oh) monitors onboard navigation and the guidance computer software.

Apollo 11 GUIDO: Steve Bales (for Lunar landing)

Flight Surgeon

Astronauts assigned to a mission receive the best medical care before launch and after the crew returns to Earth. What about during missions, you ask? Don't worry; the astronauts are in good hands. A medical doctor, known as the flight surgeon, operates a console in the MCC.

Astronauts and the flight surgeon have private conversations. These privileged communications aren't discussed with others unless there is cause for concern (an astronaut revels a medical ailment that could affect the mission, for instance).

Apollo 11 Surgeon: Dr. William (Bill) Carpentier. Dr. Carpentier was also quarantined with the astronauts when they returned to Earth.

Public Affairs Officer (PAO)

The PAO provides commentary and mission information to the media and public.

Apollo 11 PAO:

> **Jack King** was "voice" of the *Apollo 11* launch and countdown
>
> **Douglas Ward** guided listeners through the lunar landing
>
> **Jack Riley** commented during the lunar surface EVA

Data Console Setup

In the control room, four rows of consoles and monitors filled the space. Each row is lower than the one behind it so the team could see the huge projection screens mounted on the front wall.

The "trench" was the nickname for the bottom row of consoles in the MCC. In the trench were the specialists who kept the flight on the right path. Where did the previously mentioned positions sit? From top to bottom:

> **Row 1**: *PAO*
>
> **Row 2**: *Flight Director*
>
> **Row 3**: *Surgeon; CapCom*
>
> **Row 4 (The Trench)**: *GUIDO; FDO*

BEHIND THE SCENES WITH KATHERINE JOHNSON

Katherine Johnson is NASA's most famous "human computer," a group of elite female mathematicians, engineers, and scientists. Johnson was relegated to the "colored" section of human computers because of segregation. Johnson, a mathematician and physicist, was instrumental in running complex calculations that helped make the *Apollo 11* lunar mission a success.

For her work, Johnson received many honors including the Presidential Medal of Freedom (2015). The movie Hidden Figures (2016) and the book of the same name is based on Johnson and her peers' lives at NASA. In September 2017, NASA named a new research building the Katherine G. Johnson Computational Research Facility in her honor.

Johnson, born in 1918, began working for NASA in 1953 when it was still the National Advisory Committee for Aeronautics. She retired in 1986 after working 33 years for the agency.

Katherine Johnson, NASA's most famous "human computer."

The people who made the lunar landing a success didn't look for accolades. In some ways, it wasn't President Kennedy's challenge that drove them. They were scientists with a desire to put a man on the Moon to satisfy their own quest for scientific innovation.

Chapter 6

LIFT OFF

THE DATE WAS MARKED ON THE CALENDAR: JULY 16, 1969. ON this day, three pioneers would embark on a historic journey to the Moon. They wouldn't shoot directly to the Moon, though. The crew would orbit for three days. If the conditions were right, the lunar landing would take place on the afternoon of July 20.

In the weeks leading up to the launch, everything was checked and double-checked. *Apollo 11* was ready to launch. The astronauts were trained and eager to begin their journey, and the flight crew knew their roles.

President Kennedy's goal was within reach. It seemed a simple goal — according NASA's 250+ page press-kit, *Apollo 11*'s objective was to: "Perform a manned lunar landing and return." [43]

F-MINUS FIVE

You're probably familiar with the countdown leading to the launch of a spacecraft.

"T-minus 45 minutes," a voice booms.

---

43. NASA, 1969.

"T" stands for **time**, specifically the amount of time remaining before a spacecraft is scheduled to launch. In the above example, lift-off would occur in 45 minutes.

The hours and minutes before the launch are hectic and filled with excitement. But there's another equally important term: **F-Minus Five**. This important day is the fifth day before a planned mission launch. For the lunar team, F-Minus Five was Friday, July 11.

The day is significant because it's the last comprehensive medical examination for the crew. A second quick exam happens on the morning of the launch. Collins joked that, on launch day, the doctor, "... looks in one ear and if he doesn't see out the other, you go." [44]

But on July 11, the astronauts were thoroughly examined before the mission was given the green light. There's a backup crew prepared to step up in case the exams give any red-flags: James Lowell, William Anders, and Fred Haise. But everyone knew if any of the *Apollo 11* astronauts failed their medical exam, the launch wouldn't proceed at all.

A large amount of specialized training was exclusive to the primary crew. Even if NASA wanted to, it wasn't possible to switch players. They couldn't just yell, "Tag, you're it," and send in another group of astronauts.

If the mission couldn't proceed with the original crew, it would take a minimum of one month to train a replacement. It wasn't only serious ailments that could sideline an astronaut, either. Even a minor ailment like a sore throat or the 48-hour flu could derail the entire launch.

---

44. Farmer, 1970.

You might be thinking that they could just delay the launch a few days if one of the men had a tummy ache or something minor. But in the case of the lunar launch, precision mattered. NASA scientists chose the exact date and time — July 16, 1969, 9:31 a.m. — to coincide with the "lunar window." The lunar window was the ideal, but limited amount or time, when the *Apollo 11* mission could expect success.

This opening involved a lot of complex calculations — too complex for the scope of this book. Let's just say the launch date and time is not random. Here's a brief example of this type of precision at work.

It takes the Moon:

27 *days*

7 *hours*

43 *minutes* to make **1** revolution around the Earth.

The Moon's position to the Sun results in lunar days and nights. Each cycle is about 15 days. Even considering a scientist's precise calculations, it's difficult to hit the Moon. This is why NASA scheduled the lunar landing to take place on the spot they predicted the Moon would be positioned at on July 20. The anticipated spot was the peacefully named Sea of Tranquility.

There is *some* wiggle room, but not much. NASA could possibly delay the launch for about four hours in the event of minor setbacks, but for the sake of everyone at NASA's nerves, they'd prefer not to.

To make sure that the astronauts didn't pick up any pesky bugs that could sideline the mission, the crew was put in pre-launch quarantine or isolation. Only essential people are allowed to have close contact with the crew. And even those essential visitors wore masks to prevent germs from hitching a ride into outer space embedded in one of the astronauts.

The astronauts were examined by three doctors: Dr. Jack Teegan, Dr. Bill Carpentier, and Dr. Al Harter. Nurse Dee O'Hara assisted the physicians. The responsibility for the all-clear diagnosis fell on Dr. Charles Berry, Director of Medical Research and Operations.

One of O'Hara's responsibilities was handling the massive amount of paperwork associated with each mission. This included 12 pages per astronaut for the physical exams. The head-to-toe comprehensive exams began at 4:30 a.m. By the afternoon, the men were cleared for launch.

After spending time with their families in Houston over the Fourth of July weekend, the astronauts spent most of their time in the crew quarters. They spent a bit of time in the simulators, too, but at this point, they were so prepared that they could probably perform the maneuvers while dozing. They also participated in a pre-launch press conference on July 14.

The crew accommodations at NASA were windowless, but each astronaut had a bedroom with an office, and they would meet in the conference room to review plans. They had a private cook, Lew Hartzell, who prepared three meals a day for the men.

Launch Watch

As the launch date approached, people flocked to Cape Canaveral and Cocoa Beach, eager to witness first-hand this historic liftoff. Cape Canaveral is a coastal oasis located nine miles from the Kennedy Space Center. Cocoa Beach is another five miles down the road from that.

The historic event caused millions of people to pour into these beach towns in RVs and campers. The highways were frenzied with caravans of family-packed cars; boats littered the waterways. Spectators came from cities near and far.

Days before liftoff, crowds swarmed the beach and the roads, squatting to find a place to witness this moment in history. Hotels in the area were booked. Even before there was Air BnB, families in Florida rented out their sofas and other sleeping accommodations to visitors. Eventually, more than a million people would head to the Cape for the launch.

Over 1,000 law enforcement personnel (police officers, sheriff's deputies, state troopers, the U.S. Coast Guard, and the U.S. Marines) patrolled the area, making sure everyone was safe. An estimated 350,000 vehicles and boats were at the Cape on launch day.

NASA invited 20,000 VIP guests, who were flown in by helicopter and spirited away to reserved bleachers and other special locations. Dignitaries included:

- former President Lyndon Johnson and his wife, Lady Bird

- current Vice-President, Spiro Agnew

- hundreds of foreign ministers

- many celebrities including Johnny Carson (*The Tonight Show* host)

- governors, mayors, most of the U.S. Congress, and Supreme Court justices.

FAST FACT

3,497 journalists witnessed the launch. This included 812 from 54 foreign countries.

WHERE WERE THE ASTRONAUTS' FAMILIES DURING LAUNCH?

Did the astronauts' families attend the launch? Here's a rundown on who was where.

Armstrong: The commander asked his wife not to attend the launch but she insisted. In many cases, the family of an astronaut doesn't attend in case something goes wrong. For the launch, Mrs. Armstrong and the kids attended a yacht party on the Banana River hosted by North American Aviation. His parents watched from home in Ohio.

Aldrin: Mrs. Aldrin chose to watch the launch on TV at home in Texas surrounded by her kids, relatives, and friends.

Collins: Mrs. Collins also decided to watch the launch at home with family.

Apollo 11 Mission Patch

Beginning with the *Gemini V* mission, each crew designed their mission patch. The *Apollo 11* astronauts decided to make a few changes to their patch. Most notably, they decided to leave their names off the patch.

According to Collins: "We wanted to keep our three names off it because we wanted the design to be representative of everyone who had worked toward a lunar landing, and there were thousands who could take a proprietary interest in it, yet who would never see their names woven into the fabric of a patch. Further, we wanted the design to be symbolic rather than explicit." [45]

---

45. Smith, 2016.

The men also decided to use Arabic numerals (11) instead of Roman (XI). Astronaut Jim Lovell proposed the idea for the eagle. This was appropriate since the eagle is the national bird of the United States, but more so because the lunar module was named *The Eagle*.

Collins sketched the first design. He found an image of an eagle in a National Geographic book and traced it using tissue paper. Under the eagle's talons, he drew craters. The Earth peeked from behind the eagle's wings.

The crew felt that there was still something missing. NASA employee Tom Wilson suggested including an olive branch, a symbol of peace. The crew loved the idea and Collins added an olive branch in the eagle's beak.

Bob Gilruth, director of the space center, didn't like the first design. He had an issue with the eagle's talons. He felt having the eagle landing with its talons extended looked "hostile and warlike." [46] The design was altered to have the olive branch placed in the eagle's talons instead of its beak. Collins said the eagle looked uncomfortable, but Gilruth made the final decision.

The patches are embroidered and sewn into the flight and recovery suits, jackets, and other official mission gear. The spacesuits don't have embroidered patches; the patch is silkscreened onto the fabric.

Although the *Apollo 11* patch is probably one of the most easily recognizable of all NASA mission patches, there is one error in the design that was never corrected. The image of Earth against the black sky is incorrect. The patch shows a shadow on the left side of the Earth. However, when viewed from the Moon's surface, the shadow would fall on the bottom. However, as Collins said, the design was meant to be symbolic.

---

46. Smith, 2016.

The patch of the Apollo 11 mission.

THE COUNTDOWN

Armstrong, Aldrin, and Collins boarded *Apollo 11* at 6:54 a.m. From speakers placed across the sprawling 18,000-acre campus, announcer Jack King, NASA PAO and launch commentator, would describe to the world what was happening in real-time.

300 people were working in the launch control center to assure a successful liftoff. In Houston, MCC controllers waited patiently for their chance to assume control of the spacecraft.

The official countdown clock started at **T-minus 28 hours**. Here's a highlight of events leading up to the historic liftoff.

T-minus 27 hours, 30 minutes:

- Installation of the launch vehicle flight batteries

- LM stowage and cabin closeout

T-minus 21 hours:

- Top off LM super critical helium

T-minus 16 hours:

- Launch vehicle range safety checks

T-minus 11 hours, 30 minutes:

- Install launch vehicle destruct devices

T-minus 8 hours, 30 minutes:

- Astronaut backup crew arrives at spacecraft for pre-launch checks

T-minus 5 hours, 17 minutes:

- Human alarm clock Deke Slayton wakes up the crew

T-minus 5 hours, 2 minutes:

- After a quick shower and shave, crew proceeds to the exercise room for last minute medical and physical exam including measurements like temperature and weight

T-minus 4 hours, 32 minutes:

- Chef Lew has prepared the crew's last meal on Earth for the next 8 days

- On the menu: steak, eggs, toast, juice, and coffee

- While noshing, an artist sketches the crew as part of a NASA art program

T-minus 3 hours, 57 minutes:

- Suit up

Suiting Up

After breakfast, the men head to the suit room to get ready. Collins had an intravehicular spacesuit, meaning he could only wear it inside *Apollo 11* during the mission. Aldrin and Armstrong wore extravehicular suits. This specially designed gear was equipped to keep the astronauts safe when they stepped outside the LM.

The extravehicular suit has added layers of protection to shield the crew from the harsh elements in space and on the Moon. The lunar crew had a portable four-hour life support system.

The life support system consisted of a backpack with a supply of oxygen and cooling water (supplied to a cooling water garment).

The suit, portable life support system, a liquid cooling garment, and other components together comprised the Extravehicular Mobility Unit (EMU). The EMU weighed 183 pounds. By contrast, the intravehicular unit weighed only 35.6 pounds.

The men needed help getting into their spacesuits. The process went like this:

- Apply ointment

- Tape on diaper

- Attach waist-mounted urine collection device

- Attach biosensors to chest to send heart and respiration (breathing) and other medical data to flight surgeon

- Slip into constant-wear cotton garment, similar to long johns (long underwear)

- Seal and zip the suits (the suits are zipped from the back)

- Put on "Snoopy hats" — brown and white skullcaps, containing a microphone and earpiece

- Put on boots, which are wrapped in protective plastic to keep any Earth germs from hitching a ride to the Moon.

The astronauts also had snug nylon gloves underneath the suit's gloves that were locked to the suit's arms. The final touch was donning the fish-bowl-shaped helmets, which were then locked to the suits neckrings.

FAST FACT

ILC Dover (based in Delaware) made the spacesuits. Hamilton Standard (now UTC Aerospace Systems) provided some of the critical systems for the mission, including the life support system.

"When we are all three ready, we plug ourselves into portable oxygen containers, and carrying them like heavy suitcases, we begin the long walk down to the transfer van, which in turn will take us to the launch pad," Collins wrote in his autobiography, *Carrying the Fire*. [47]

The Apollo 11 crew heading to the van to be taken to the launch pad.

As the men head to the launch pad, the hallway is lined with well-wishers. Some are friends and co-workers. Many more were strangers, according to Collins. With so many people working on the mission, Collins admitted they recognized only a fraction of people. Commander Neil Armstrong led the crew procession.

T-minus 3 hours, 7 minutes:

As the men exit the building, a throng of TV cameras and photographers, clamoring for a last pre-launch image, greet the three voyagers. Collins said

47. Collins, 1974.

they gave "... jerky little waves to the photographers as we walk stiff-legged toward the van." [48]

Once inside the van, the vehicle bumps along an eight-mile route. Although it's still very early, the street is already lined with tourists in their cars, crawling toward the launch pad. But they speed past the cars, one lane cleared for the important cargo.

PERSONAL PREFERENCE KIT

NASA allows each astronaut to bring special items on their space journey. These items are called a Personal Preference Kit (PPK). The kit is a small bag with items of special significance to the astronaut. What were some of the items in the *Apollo 11* astronauts PPKs? According to Collins: "... prayers, poems, medallions, coins, flags, envelopes, brooches, tie pins, insignia, cuff links, rings, and even one diaper pin." [49]

T-minus 2 hours, 55 minutes:

After emerging from the van, the men ambled to the elevator. This ride would take them to where their ride to Moon waited. *Apollo 11* would liftoff from Launchpad 39A.

The men noticed an eerie silence. True, it was difficult to hear within the bubble of their helmet, but something else was different. Then they realized the launch pad was a ghost town. During training, the pad had been a beehive of activity. Now, all the worker bees were absent. They had done their job and there was only a handful needed for the final preparations.

---

48. Collins, 1974.
49. Collins, 1974.

There was one person with the astronauts, Deke Slayton. He'd rode with the team in the van and walked them to the elevator, but now it was time for him to leave. "Have a good trip," he told them. [50]

T-minus 2 hours, 40 minutes, 40 seconds:

The Public Affairs Officer has been providing public commentary. As the liftoff approaches, he continues to keep the public informed.

> **PAO:** "*At this time, the prime crew for Apollo 11 has boarded the high-speed elevator from inside the A level of the mobile launcher which is the second level inside the launcher ... Shortly, we'll expect astronauts Neil Armstrong and Michael Collins to come across Swing Arm 9, the Apollo access arm, and proceed to the white room and stand by to board the spacecraft. The third member of the crew, astronaut Edwin Aldrin, will be the last one to board the spacecraft, will stand by in the elevator seated in a chair while his two comrades first board the spacecraft ... Once Armstrong, who sits in the left-hand seat, and Collins, who will sit in the right-hand seat during lift-off, are aboard, then Aldrin will be called and he will take his seat, the middle seat in the spacecraft.*" [51]

Once the astronauts were settled, there were a few last minute checks by backup crewmember Fred Haise. Then the crew was left alone in the CM. Outside the close-out crew still had work to complete before the launch.

Inside the hatch, the *Apollo 11* astronauts performed their own checks while perched on top of the monster Saturn rocket. Armstrong and Aldrin

---

50. Barbree, 2014.
51. Woods, 2017. Please note: All quoted commentary for the remainder of chapter from this source.

had the most to do. Collins said he had time to think and daydream: "Here I am, a white male, age 38, height 5 feet, 11 inches, weight 165 pounds, salary $17,000 per annum, resident of a Texas suburb, with black spot on my roses, state of mind unsettled, about to be shot off to the moon." [52] It *was* a lot process but it was too late to back out now.

T-minus 2 hours, 55 seconds:

PAO: *"We're approaching the two-hour mark in our countdown and we appear to be proceeding satisfactorily at this time."*

T-minus 1 hour, 55 minutes, 55 seconds:

PAO: *"We're proceeding with the countdown with the Apollo 11 mission at this time and it's going satisfactorily. At this point, the spacecraft Commander Neil Armstrong is in the process of working the Emergency Detection System test. Weather is Go."*

T-minus 1 hour, 30 minutes, 55 seconds:

PAO: *"All elements are Go with the countdown at this time ... We're winding up this important Emergency Detection System test that Neil Armstrong has been participating in ... the close-out crew now placing the Boost Protective Cover over the hatch ... in the firing room, the launch vehicle test team's still keeping a close eye on the status of the propellants aboard the Saturn V launch vehicle ... All aspects Go. The weather is very satisfactory for launch this morning. A thin cloud cover about 15,000 feet. Temperature at launch time expected to be about 85 degrees."*

---

52. Collins, 1974.

T-minus 1 hour, 11 minutes:

The close-out crew will soon complete the last system checks. After they exit, the Apollo access swing-arm will move back 12 degrees (about 5 feet) from the hatch. The swing-arm remains in this position until the 5-minute mark, when it is fully retracted to its fall-back position. It remains in the stand-by position so that in case of an emergency, support crew could quickly move the arm back to the hatch and the astronauts could easily escape.

T-minus 50 minutes, 51 seconds:

> **PAO:** *"All elements reporting ready at this point in the countdown ... in about 30 seconds that big swing arm that has been attached to the spacecraft up to now will be moved back to a parked position some 5 feet away from the spacecraft."*

T-minus 42 minutes:

- The launch escape system is checked and armed

T-minus 40 minutes:

- Final launch vehicle range safety test

After the final launch vehicle range safety test is conducted, the astronauts are asked how things are going. Armstrong reports: "We're very comfortable. It's a very nice morning."

MCC Flight Director Cliff Charlesworth breaks in to say his team is ready to assume control of the vehicle as soon as it clears the tower.

T-minus 30 minutes:

- The launch vehicle power transfer test is conducted

- The LM is switched to internal power source

T-minus 16 minutes:

PAO: *"All still going well with the countdown at this time ... Once we get down to the 3-minute-and-10-second mark in the countdown, we'll go on an automatic sequence. As far as the launch vehicle is concerned, all aspects from there on down will be automatic, run by the ground master computer here in the firing room."*

T-minus 15 minutes:

The spacecraft is now on full internal power. Armstrong and Aldrin have armed their rotational hand controllers. The Emergency Detection System is ready. The system will warn the astronauts if there's trouble with the Saturn V during flight.

T-minus 6 minutes:

A final status check of the vehicle is conducted. The mission is still on time for the planned launch. The checks are running smoothly. The firing room reports the mission is still a Go.

T-minus 5 minutes:

- The Apollo access arm is fully retracted.

T-minus 3 minutes, 25 seconds:

PAO: *"Firing command coming in now ... T-minus 3 minutes and counting ... We're on an automatic sequence as the master computer supervises hundreds of events occurring over these last few minutes."*

T-minus 50 seconds:

- The launch vehicle transfers to internal power.

T-minus 20 seconds:

PAO: *"Twenty seconds and counting ... T- minus 15 seconds, guidance is internal. Twelve, 11, 10, 9, ignition sequence starts, 8,7,6, 5, 4, 3, 2, 1, 0, all engine [sic] running. We have LIFTOFF! We have a lift-off, 32 minutes past the hour. Lift-off on Apollo 11."*

====== FAST FACT ======

PAO Jack King was so excited he said, "all engine running" instead of "all engines running".

Apollo 11 blasts off, the Saturn V trailing a skirt of fire. Four seconds into the mission we hear the voice of Apollo commander Neil Armstrong.

000:00:04 Armstrong: *"Roger. Clock."*

PAO: *"Tower cleared."*

At this point LCC relinquishes control to MCC.

The Apollo 11 launch.

FAST FACT:

Once the Saturn V and *Apollo 11* began to rise, the time terminology changed to GET (General Elapsed Time) or MET (Mission Elapsed Time).

After lift off, the crew flies upside down for two and half hours before being shot toward the Moon. This is called a *holding orbit*. Their heads point toward Earth and their feet toward the sky. This is to allow the sextant (a navigational aid) to point at the stars. Collins has to take a few readings to make sure the navigation equipment is functioning properly before they can safely leave Earth's orbit.

The crew spend hours cycling thorough a series of procedures. It's mostly serious talk, with periodic light banter, like this exchange between Armstrong and Aldrin:

> **000:46:06** Aldrin: *"It's a little on the chilly side in the cabin. Would you like ..."*
>
> **000:46:08** Armstrong: *"Feels comfortable to me."*
>
> **000:46:09** Aldrin: *"... would you like it a little warmer, anybody?"*
>
> **000:46:16** Armstrong: *"It sure doesn't look, sure doesn't feel like - Actually, it may be a little - it may be a little warm."*
>
> **000:46:20** Aldrin: *"Well, my - my feet are a little chilly. See, it's 47."*

The Saturn's job is almost complete. Collins has to separate the Command and Service Modules from the Saturn V. He moves a safe distance, then turns around to face the launcher. Once the LM separates from the Saturn, MCC changes its trajectory to miss the Moon. It will then float in space until completely running out of fuel (it's almost empty at this point).

After they say good-bye to the Saturn and drift toward the Moon, the men remove their bulky, pressurized space suits and change into two-piece nylon jump suits.

——— *FAST FACT* ———————————————

A record-setting 600 million people watched the launch in person or on TV.

As *Apollo 11* drifts, the crew has a few navigation tasks to complete before retiring for the night. The PAO continues to brief listeners on what's happening aboard the spacecraft, even as the crew slept.

014:06:00

PAO: "*The mission is progressing very smoothly. All spacecraft systems are functioning normally at this time, and the Flight Surgeon reports that all three crewmen appear to be sleeping. For Commander Neil Armstrong and Lunar Module Pilot Buzz Aldrin, they appeared to begin sleeping about 5 minutes ago. Command module Pilot Mike Collins has been asleep for about an additional 30 minutes to an hour. At the present time, Apollo 11 is 66,554 nautical miles from Earth and travelling at a speed of about seventy thousand - or rather 7,095 feet per second, which would be about 4,800 miles an hour.*"

With the crew sound asleep, Day One of the lunar mission comes to an end.

APOLLO 11 ASTRONAUT SALARIES

Have you ever wondered how much money the astronauts made? Here's a rundown of what each astronaut made in 1969 and its 2017 equivalent.

Armstrong: The commander received an annual salary of $30,054. This was based on a civil servant GS-16 Step 7 pay schedule.

In 2017: Armstrong would make $202,122.57.

Collins: As a U.S. Air Force Lieutenant, Collins made $17,147.36.

In 2017: Collins would bring in $115,321.37 annually.

Aldrin: U.S. Air Force Colonel Buzz Aldrin received a salary of $ 18,622.54.

In 2017: Aldrin would receive $125,242.55 a year.

Chapter 7

THE *EAGLE* HAS LANDED

AS THE CREW SLEPT, A MEDICAL DEVICE MONITORED THEIR vitals signs. The transmitted information crawls across the flight surgeon's console. Mission controllers continue to watch the onboard navigation equipment to ensure *Apollo 11* remains on the right path. The PAO keeps the public informed of the spacecraft's position relative to Earth and the status of the astronauts.

APOLLO 11 MISSION: DAY TWO

After the crew's sleep period and a freeze-dried breakfast, the CapCom contacts the voyagers. It's time to begin day two in space. With no time for pleasantries, the crew and the CapCom get down to business. The astronauts perform a series of checks, tasks, and maneuvers as directed by Mission Control.

As mentioned earlier, an astronaut always staffs the CapCom console. Much of the technical jargon communicated between MCC and the spacecraft is something only a trained astronaut would understand. Here's an example:

CapCom: "*Apollo 11*, this is Houston. Midcourse Correction number 2. SPS/G&N; 63059; plus 0.97, minus 0.20; GET ignition

026:44:57.92; plus 0011.8, minus 0000.3, plus 0017.7; roll, 277, 355, 015; Noun 44, Block is N/A; Delta-V$_T$ 0021.3, 00:3, 0016.8; sextant star 30, 208.2, 37.0. The rest of the PAD is N/A. GDC align, Vega and Deneb; roll align 007, 144, 068. No ullage. LM weight: 33302."[53]

To complicate matters further, Armstrong has to correctly repeat back exactly what the CapCom said.

The crew continues to work diligently their first day in orbit. The exchanges between the MCC and the crew are mainly serious, technical business. But just before they break for lunch, they have this funny interchange:

028:42:08 CapCom: "Is that music I hear in the background?"

028:42:15 Collins: "Buzz is singing."

028:42:16 CapCom: "Okay."

028:42:31 Collins: "Pass me the sausage, man."

After lunch, the crew returns to work. They spend time observing the view of Earth from space and snapping pictures. They also use the onboard camera for a TV broadcast. Day two finally winds down and the crew settles in for a 10-hour sleep cycle.

---

53. NASA, 2015. NOTE: Unless otherwise indicated, all quotes & transcript info. in this chapter from same source.

WHAT DID THE ASTRONAUTS EAT IN SPACE?

The voyagers had a selection of freeze-dried morsels to choose from. Before eating, the food had to be rehydrated. Adding water to the bag and kneading it for about three minutes rehydrated the item. Then the neck of the container was cut open and the food squeezed into the astronaut's mouth.

The crew had three meals each day and pantry snack items.

Let's look at a few menu examples:

Breakfast	**Lunch**	**Dinner**
Peaches	*Frankfurter*	*Salmon Salad*
Bacon Squares (8)	*Applesauce*	*Chicken and Rice*
Strawberry Cubes (4)	*Chocolate Pudding*	*Sugar Cookie Cubes (6)*
Grape Drink	*Orange-Grapefruit Drink*	*Cocoa*
Orange Drink		*Pineapple-Grapefruit Drink*

The snack pantry contained some of the same items from the daily menus including:

- Peaches
- Cereal cubes
- Tuna salad
- Soups/stews

- Banana and chocolate pudding
- Drinks/punch
- Coffee/cocoa
- Bread

- Brownies
- Candy

APOLLO 11 MISSION: DAY THREE

Rise and shine sleepy heads. The PAO informs listeners that the crew has overslept, but now they are stirring. 48 hours into the mission, *Apollo 11* is drifting 160,760 nautical miles from Earth. The scheduled 10-hour rest period has yawned and stretched into 11 hours. They receive their morning wake-up call from Houston. The CapCom reports all systems are functioning properly.

Two of the voyagers — Aldrin and Collins — run through a series of tasks and updates. After the morning tasks are complete, the two have breakfast. Armstrong hasn't appeared yet. The CapCom has the morning newspaper and wants to know if the guys are interested in what's happening back on Earth. They tell him to go ahead.

The CapCom recounts mundane items like the weather, sports scores, and an upcoming Senate vote relating to income taxes. Then this interesting item:

> **053:56:39 CapCom:** "And in Corby, England, an Irishman, John Coyle has won the world's porridge eating championship by consuming 23 bowls of instant oatmeal in a 10-minute time limit from a field of 35 other competitors. Over."

This item triggers an interesting chat:

> **053:57:55 Collins:** "I'd like to enter Aldrin in the oatmeal eating contest next time."

> **053:58:00 CapCom:** "Is he pretty good at that?"

> **053:58:04 Collins:** "He's doing his share up here."

053:58:13 CapCom "Let's see. You all just finished a meal not long ago, too, didn't you?"

053:58:20 Aldrin: "I'm still eating."

053:58:27 Collins: "He's on his — he's on his 19th bowl."

Later the crew decides to check out the LM for the first time. They also decide to have an unplanned TV transmission tour of the lunar module's interior.

57 hours into the mission, the PAO informs listeners that Apollo *11* is 179,490 miles from Earth, and the spacecraft is traveling at a speed of 3,121 feet per second. In three hours, *Apollo 11* will pass into the *lunar sphere of influence*. This means that the Moon's gravity will primarily control the trajectory or path of the spacecraft. With another busy day behind them, the astronauts settle down for the night.

DID THE APOLLO 11 ASTRONAUTS SEE A UFO?

Could the astronauts have witnessed a UFO? The crew noticed an unexplained "tumbling, flashing object." Armstrong thought maybe it was the abandoned third stage of the Saturn V rocket. He contacted Houston and asked if they could verify the location of the launcher. After a pause, the CapCom said the S-IVB was 6,000 miles from their current location. At that distance it was unlikely what they observed was the abandoned launcher. The identity of the flashing object remains a mystery. However, there's a lot of space debris floating around up there. One theory is the "UFO" could have been one of the SLA panels that covered the LM during launch.

APOLLO 11 MISSION: DAY FOUR

The crew sleep late again. After rousing, they begin their day with the usual series of checks, counter-checks, maneuvers, and housekeeping. There is periodic loss of signal and the PAO does an excellent job keeping listeners informed of when the LOS will occur and when MCC regains signal. The PAO's main job is keeping the public informed of what's happening on the spacecraft and in the MCC. A recorder was on board *Columbia* to record the crew's conversations during LOS.

As the spacecraft drifts, the crew glimpse the site of the lunar landing for the first time. The commander reports "... the pictures and maps brought back by *Apollos 8* and *10* have given us a very good preview of what to look at here. It looks very much like the pictures, but like the difference between watching a real football game and one on TV. There's no substitute for actually being here."

83 hours into the mission, the PAO informs listeners that the LM is transmitting data to MCC displays. This comes after a communications check by Aldrin. Satisfied that all is well, the LM is powered down. The crew retires for the night to rest for the big day ahead.

APOLLO 11 MISSION: DAY FIVE, LUNAR LANDING

On lunar landing day, the crew receives a wake-up call from CapCom Ronald Evans. The call comes about two minutes before the next scheduled LOS. After the signal is acquired again, the CapCom reads a few newspaper headlines to the crew. He reports that many churches around the world are keeping the *Apollo 11* voyagers in their prayers. President Nixon is holding a worship service at the White House and dedicating it to the mission.

To lighten the mood, the men are informed about a particularly interesting headline. The crew is warned to look out for a lovely girl with a big rabbit. Supposedly — according to an ancient Chinese legend — a girl named Chang-O has lived on the Moon for 4,000 years. She was banished after stealing the pill of immortality from her husband. Apparently, her companion was a large, unnamed rabbit. Collins response: "Okay. We'll keep a close eye out for the bunny girl."

FAST FACT

How many hours did each astronaut sleep the night before the lunar landing? Armstrong slept five and a half hours; Collins nodded off for six hours; and Aldrin dozed for five hours.

During the next LOS, the PAO gives an update. The mission is progressing smoothly. Aldrin and Armstrong begin checking out and activating the LM. During revolution 13, the LM will undock from the CSM.

As *Apollo 11* continues to orbit, back at MCC the flight controllers assess their systems and report their findings to Flight Director Gene Kranz. He will make the "Go" or "No Go" decision on undocking based on information received from his team.

99 hours into the mission, the crew receives the "Go" for undocking.

099:25:08 Aldrin: "Roger. Understand."

100:18:01 Armstrong: "Roger. Eagle's undocked."

100:18:03 CapCom: "Roger. How does it look, Neil?"

100:18:04 Armstrong: "The Eagle has wings."

And just like that, the *Eagle* leaves the nest. As the scheduled time for the lunar landing approaches, the space around Mission Control becomes crowded with NASA dignitaries. Among those in the viewing room are:

- Dr. Thomas Paine, *NASA Administrator*

- Dr. Abe Silverstein, *Director of NASA's Lewis Research Center*

- Rocco Petrone, *Director of Launch Operations at Kennedy Space Center*

- Dr. Wernher von Braun, *Director at Marshall Space Flight Center*

- Astronauts Tom Stafford, Gene Cernan, Jim McDivitt, and John Glenn

- Dr. Kurt Debus, *Director of the Kennedy Space Center*

- Dr. Edgar Cortright, *Director of the Langley Research Center.*

The control room was also flooded with people. Including:

- Astronauts Pete Conrad, Fred Haise, Jim Lovell, and Bill Anders

- Dr. Robert Gilruth, *Director of the Manned Spacecraft Center*

- General Sam Phillips, *Director of the Apollo Program*

- Chris Kraft, *Director of Flight Operations at the Manned Spacecraft Center.*

As the clock ticks toward the landing hour, the atmosphere in MCC becomes quiet. Kranz instructs everyone to sit down and start preparing for the historic event.

ONE SMALL STEP

Finally, the big moment arrives; it is time to make history. Krantz gives a pep talk to his controllers:

> "Today is our day, and the hopes and dreams of the entire world are with us ... In the next hour, we will do something that has never been done before — we will land an American on the Moon ... We worked long hours and had some tough times, but we have mastered our work ... Good luck, and God bless us today!" [54]

Then he locks the doors, which is normal procedure during all critical missions.

The selected landing spot in the Sea of Tranquility was chosen because photos showed that the location appeared free of boulders and craters. On the day of the lunar landing, the sun would be in an ideal position for viewing the surface details without too much shadow or glare. There's only one day in each lunar cycle when this happens. For this cycle, July 20 was that day.

The mission is progressing nicely with one exception: there is a malfunction in the communication system. While waiting to give the "Go" or "No Go" for descent, flight controllers lose contact with *Eagle*. The solution is to relay messages to Collins onboard *Columbia*, who will then pass the message to his fellow astronauts if they don't respond to Houston.

---

54. Kranz, 2000.

A map depicting the Sea of Tranquility.

Kranz polls the flight controllers and issues a "Go" for descent.

> **102:28:08 CapCom**: "*Eagle*, Houston. If you read, you are a go for powered descent."

After a period of silence, Collins jumps in.

> **102:28:18 Collins:** "*Eagle*, *Columbia*. They just gave you a go for powered descent ... *Eagle* do you read *Columbia*?"

102:28:48 Aldrin: "We read you."

102:28: 51 CapCom: "Eagle, Houston. We read you now. You're go for PDI."

(PDI stands for Powered Descent Initiate.)

102:28:57 Aldrin: "Roger."

The men continue their descent. The communication link continues to malfunction, causing MCC to sometimes relay messages through Collins.

The time for the most important decision of the mission has arrived. Kranz polls his controllers again. Was the mission a "Go" or "No Go" for landing? The crew receives a thumbs up.

The *Eagle* begins its descent. There is a collective holding of breath in the control room and around the world. Then there's a snag. Armstrong isn't happy with the terrain of the planned landing spot. The computer system is steering the spacecraft to a location filled with boulders. Some of the rocks were as big as small cars. "I was tempted to land, but my better judgment took over," said Armstrong. [55]

The commander takes manual control of the module. The LM skims over the Moon's surface as Armstrong searches for a better spot to land. There is now an even more urgent problem: the fuel gauge is inching toward empty. If Armstrong doesn't touch down soon, he will have to fire the ascent engine and abort the mission.

---

55. Nelson, 2009.

In Mission Control, flight controllers are biting their fingernails. It's taking too long for the *Eagle* to land and they don't know why because Armstrong is radio silent. The only thing they know for certain is that the fuel will run out soon.

The air in MCC is thick with anticipation as the fuel percentage melts away. The Eagle has 60 seconds of fuel remaining when a warning light comes on. Aldrin says they are still about 100 feet from the ground.

He'd been calm so far, trusting Armstrong to get them down safely, but now he's concerned. "But what could I do? Could I say 'Neil, hurry up, get it on the ground?'" Aldrin said. [56] He doesn't want to do that because he feels it might make Armstrong more excitable and nervous. And now they are at a point where firing the ascent engine wouldn't help. If they run out of fuel, the men will crash into the Moon.

Armstrong finally sees a clear spot. He has about 17 seconds of fuel remaining.

Next, MCC hears the commander's ever-calm voice:

> **102:45:58 (3:17 p.m. CST): Armstrong:** "Engine arm is off. Houston, *Tranquility Base* here. The *Eagle* has landed."

—— *FAST FACT* ————

During the lunar phase of the mission, call sign changed to "*Tranquility Base*".

---

56. Nelson, 2009.

There is a collective sigh of relief followed by spontaneous cheering. The United States had just made history by landing two men on the Moon. But the mission isn't over yet.

Yes, man has landed on the Moon, but is it safe to *stay* on the Moon? Kranz surveys the flight controllers for what's called a "T-1 stay/no stay".

Armstrong and Aldrin have their own system checks to complete. These checks will decide if they can remain on the Moon. Thankfully, all tests and checks from MCC and the astronauts are positive. The crew have two hours to perform their EVAs.

The plan for the mission had changed from what NASA officials had visualized. This was the old plan:

1. Armstrong and Aldrin would land the LM.

2. The crew would perform a system check on the spacecraft.

3. The astronauts would sleep for four hours.

4. After their rest period, the voyagers would perform the EVAs.

However, the crew felt it was a better idea to perform the EVAs first and then sleep; NASA agreed. The decision was made before the launch. Another benefit of an earlier walk was being able to broadcast during primetime (at 8 p.m. CST).

The explorers next disconnect from the LM's port. They check to see if they have everything.

- Personal Life Support System ✔

- Backpacks ✔

- Oxygen Purge System ✔

- Data Cards ✔

- Scissors ✔

- Penlights ✔

- Boots ✔

- Overshoes ✔

- Gloves ✔

109:15:45 Aldrin: "Okay. About ready to go down and get some Moon rock?"

―――― **FAST FACT** ――――――――――――――――――――――

An estimated one billion people watched the lunar landing.

Getting out of the LM isn't an easy feat. Armstrong starts the complicated process of exiting through the hatch by getting down on his knees with his back to Aldrin. Next, he maneuvers his feet toward the hatch.

109:16:49 Aldrin: "Okay ... Forward and up; now you are clear. Little bit toward me. Straight down. To your left a little bit. Plenty of room. Okay, you're lined up nicely. Toward me a little bit, down. Okay. Now you're clear. You're catching the first hinge ..."

109:18:28 Armstrong: "How am I doing?"

109:18:29 Aldrin: "You're doing fine."

109:19:16 Armstrong: "Okay. Houston, I'm on the porch."

109:19:20 CapCom: "Roger, Neil."

The CapCom informs Armstrong that everyone is waiting for the TV signal to come through. Soon, a picture appears on the screen.

109:22:48 CapCom: "Okay. Neil, we can see you coming down the ladder now."

109:22:59 Armstrong: "Okay. I just checked getting back up to that first step ..."

109:23:10 CapCom: "Roger. We copy."

109:23:38 Armstrong: "I'm at the foot of the ladder. The LM footpads are only depressed in the surface about 1 or 2 inches, although the surface appears to be very, very fine-grained, as you get close to it. It's almost like a powder."

109:24:12 Armstrong: "Okay. I'm going to step off the LM now."

109:24:23 Armstrong: "That's one small step for [a] man; one giant leap for mankind."

With that simple statement, Neil Armstrong becomes the first man to walk on the Moon. The time was 9:56:20 p.m. CST.

Neil Armstrong on the moon.

FAST FACT

Did listeners mishear Armstrong's iconic words when he stepped on the Moon? Armstrong later reported that he said "... step for **a** man ..." However, it seems the whole world heard "... one small step for man ..."

Over the years, people have examined the audio transcripts and most say they can't hear the "a". Armstrong admitted it might have been inaudible. He said he planned to say "a" and believes he did.

Once on the Moon, Armstrong reports that the lunar surface is fine and powdery, like charcoal. He doesn't have any problems moving around. He remarks it is even easier than in the simulations. Armstrong notices the descent engine didn't leave a crater. The ground is level, he says. Now, it is almost time for his companion to join him. But first, Armstrong has to take some pictures and get a few rock samples.

109:26:54 Armstrong: "Okay, Buzz, we ready to bring down the camera?"

109:26:59 Aldrin: "I'm all ready."

109:27:13 Armstrong: "Okay. It's quite dark here in the shadow and a little hard for me to see that I have good footing. I'll work my way over into the sunlight here without looking directly into the Sun."

109:28:17 Armstrong: "Looking up at the LM ... I'm standing directly in the shadow now, looking up at Buzz in the window. And I can see everything quite clearly. The light is sufficiently bright, backlighted into the front of the LM, that everything is very clearly visible."

109:30:53 Armstrong: "I'll step out and take some of my first pictures here."

109:34:54 Aldrin: "That looks beautiful from here, Neil."

109:34:56 Armstrong: "It has a stark beauty all its own. It's like much of the high desert of the United States. It's different, but it's very pretty out here."

Aldrin is anxious to join the party.

109:38:41 Aldrin: "Okay. Are you ready for me to come out?"

109:38:42 Armstrong: "Yeah. Just standby a second."

109:39:07 Aldrin: "All right."

109:39:11 Armstrong: "All set."

Armstrong finishes and tells Aldrin to make sure the backup camera is in the correct position. Then he guides his friend down the ladder.

109:39:57 Armstrong: "Okay ... Your toes are about to come over the sill ... There you go; you're clear."

109:40:18 Aldrin: "Okay. You need a little bit of arching of the back to come down. How far are my feet from the edge?"

109:40:27 Armstrong: "Okay. You're right at the edge of the porch."

109:40:30 Aldrin: "Okay ... Helmet comes up and clears the bulkhead without any trouble at all."

109:40:48 Armstrong: "Looks good."

Aldrin stops for a moment. He backs up and partially closes the hatch, making sure not to lock it. He jokes that the LM was going to be their home for the next few hours and he didn't want it damaged by the Moon's elements.

109:41:56 Aldrin: "I'm on the top step ... It's a very simple matter to hop down from one step to the next."

109:42:18 Armstrong: "Yes. I found I could be very comfortable, and walking is also very comfortable."

109:42:28 Armstrong: "You've got three more steps and then a long one."

109:42:42 Aldrin: "Okay. I'm going to leave that one foot up there and both hands down to about the fourth rung up."

109:42:50 Armstrong: "There you go."

Aldrin has about an inch to go and then he too will be on the lunar surface.

109:43:16 Aldrin: "Beautiful view!"

109:43:18 Armstrong: "Isn't that something! Magnificent sight out here."

109:43:24 Aldrin: "Magnificent desolation."

They both remark on the fine powder of the Moon's surface. Armstrong says he can kick it up easily. Aldrin says the moon dust bounces when you kick it. He also agrees moving around is easy and can reach down without any problems. He also notices that the engine didn't leave craters.

With not much time for sightseeing, the next step is unveiling the plaque the crew will leave on the Moon.

109:52:40 Armstrong: "For those who haven't read the plaque, we'll read the plaque that's on the front landing gear of this LM. First, there's two hemispheres, one showing each of the two hemispheres of the Earth. Underneath it says, "Here Men from the planet Earth first set foot upon the Moon, July 1969 A.D. We came in peace for all mankind."

Pictures of the plaque left on the moon.

The plaque also has the crew and the president's signature on it. After the unveiling, the men perform EVAs and set up a U.S. flag. They have so much to do and so little time to do it. The experience of being on the Moon is indescribable. Armstrong remarks that they feel like five-year-old boys in a candy store. But they have a job to do.

Both astronauts are now on the Moon. The CapCom informs the crew that a special guest has a few words to say. The caller is President Richard Nixon phoning from the Oval Office in the White House. The president remarks: "... this certainly has to be the most historic telephone call ever made."

He continue: "I just can't tell you how proud we all are of what you have done ... For every American, this has to be the proudest day of our lives. And for people all over the world, I am sure they, too, join with Americans in recognizing what an immense feat this is ... For one priceless moment in the whole history of man, all the people on this Earth are truly one; one in their pride in what you have done, and one in our prayers that you will return safely to Earth."

Armstrong thanks the president for his kind words. He says it is an honor for the astronauts to participate in the mission. Aldrin adds that he is looking forward to meeting with the president when they return to Earth.

After speaking with President Nixon, the men collect more samples and perform additional EVAs. They collect 50 pounds of lunar soil, dust, and rock samples that are packed in sealed containers.

FAST FACT

Armstrong spent 2 hours, 14 minutes on the Moon; Aldrin spent 1 hour, 44 minutes.

It has been a historic but long day. With only five hours available for sleep before lift off, the duo says goodnight to Houston. But they have trouble sleeping, partly because of the excitement of what had just happened and partly because it was reportedly freezing in The *Eagle*.

Chapter 8

RETURN TO EARTH

IT WOULD HAVE BEEN NICE IF THE CREW HAD MORE TIME TO explore, but they had to get ready to rendezvous with the CM. They leave behind five mementos for the deceased astronauts, three American and two Soviet: Gus Grissom, Ed White, Roger Chaffee, Vladimin Komarov and Yuri Gagarin.

124 hours and 22 minutes after leaving Earth, Armstrong and Aldrin launches from the lunar surface. "The Eagle has wings," Armstrong remarks. [57]

RENDEZVOUS

The PAO reports that at 129:51:00 the *Eagle* successfully rendezvoused with *Columbia*.

Collins wrote in his autobiography, *Carrying the Fire,* that the first person to come though was Aldrin. "I grab his head," he said, "a hand on each temple, and am about to give him a smooch on the forehead, as a parent

---

57. NASA, 2017. NOTE: Unless otherwise noted, quotes and transcript info for this chapter from same source.

might greet an errant child; but then embarrassed, I think better of it and grab his hand, then Neil's." [58]

They spend a few minutes horsing around, getting reacquainted, but then it's all business. He helps his mates transfer their samples and equipment from the LM.

The next order of business is to separate the LM from the CM. "When the time comes to jettison *Eagle*, I flip the necessary switches, there is a small bang, and away she goes, backing off with stately grace," said Collins.[59]

He's happy to see her go but Armstrong and Aldrin seem sad.

Apollo 11 will have to continue orbiting for a while. Mission Control has to give the "Go" for trans-Earth injection. This maneuver will separate the LM from the CM and send the astronauts home.

Once the crew settles down, the CapCom reads highlights of the morning news. He reports that the White House is receiving a steady flow of congratulatory messages. Many of the messages are coming from world leaders like Great Britain's Prime Minister and the King of Belgium. Russian Premier Alexei Kosygin and the cosmonauts also send well wishes.

The successful mission is front-page news in papers in the United States and abroad. *The New York Times* sell all 950,000 copies of their first printing. They plan to reprint the issue as a special edition.

---

58. Collins, 1974.
59. Collins, 1974.

How do the wives feel? According to reports:

Mrs. Armstrong: "The evening was unbelievably perfect. It is an honor and a privilege to share with my husband, the crew, the Manned Spacecraft Center, the American public and all mankind, the magnificent experience of the beginning of lunar exploration."

Mrs. Collins: "It was fantastically marvelous."

Mrs. Aldrin: "It was hard to think it was real until the men actually moved, after the moon touchdown, I wept because I was so happy."

The crew finally receive a "Go" for injection. They will start the maneuver at the beginning of the next revolution (their 31st).

As *Apollo 11* heads home, the weather bureau is on alert. The agency closely monitors any adverse condition near the landing spot. There is a tropical storm in the area, but Claudia was 2,300 miles east of splashdown, so her presence isn't expected to cause any problems.

When *Apollo 11* is about 174,000 nautical miles from Earth, the Moon releases its gravitational grip. The crew is back in the Earth's sphere of influence.

The crew is wide-awake after getting about eight hours of sleep. Along with their morning coffee, they receive their last news blast while in space.

CapCom: "Only four nations, Communist China, North Korea, North Vietnam, and Albania, have not yet informed their citizens of your flight and landing on the moon ... We've had rain several times here in the Houston area. Today it is cloudy and more showers are expected ... the Baseball Writers Association of America named Babe Ruth the greatest ball player of all time. Joe DiMaggio was named the greatest living ball player ..."

The CapCom also have a bit of weird news to share. In Memphis, Tennessee, Mr. And Mrs. Eddie Lee McGhee, have named their new daughter "Module." Mrs. McGhee reported it was her husband's idea. He wanted the baby named Lunar Module McGhee, but was willing to compromise.

Later, the astronauts have their last TV broadcast. Collins says they haven't rehearsed what they will say or do. He adds that they don't particularly enjoy the broadcasts. Armstrong shows the packed boxes of rocks. Aldrin demonstrates food preparation by "... slopping ham spread on a piece of bread." [60] He ends his segment by spinning a small can in midair to demonstrate the principle of gyroscopic action.

Collins demonstrates weightlessness in space by showing how astronauts drink water in zero gravity. They end their last broadcast by showing an image of Earth from *Columbia's* window.

After a TV broadcast, the crew settle down for their last nocturnal sleep cycle. Although good weather is expected, the site of the original splashdown is moved 215 miles northeast. The adjustment was made so the recovery ship — the USS *Hornet* — could arrive in Hawaii four or five hours earlier than scheduled.

SPLASHDOWN

After eight days in outer space, *Apollo 11* splashes down in Pacific Ocean. They land 812 nautical miles southwest of Hawaii. The rescue vessel, USS *Hornet,* is 12 nautical miles away.

---

60. Collins, 1974.

Apollo 11 splashdown in the Pacific Ocean.

The recovery swimmers are ready to retrieve the voyagers once the CM stabilizes. The PAO assures everyone listening that the crew was in excellent condition. A floatation collar is attached to the spacecraft and a swimmer waits in a raft next to the astronauts. He's brought a biological isolation garment (BIG) for each astronaut. The BIG is a protective measure to make sure the crew doesn't bring back any harmful germs from the moon.

The BIGs are made of rubber and zipped up the front. The suit has a hood and a visor with a filtered facemask.

The swimmer also has his own BIG. His first task is to spray the CM hatch and top deck with a decontaminate. The solution would help disinfect the module. He then passes the BIGs to the crew. Once they are dressed and have exited the CM, the swimmer scrubs down the CM with the disinfectant. Then he scrubs the astronauts' BIGs.

The men wait in a raft until a helicopter lifts the bundle and deposits them on the USS *Hornet*. The CM is also lifted and flown to the waiting recovery vessel.

RECOVERY

After the crew has been recovered, they are whisked to a mobile quarantine facility (a small trailer). Stripping off their BIGs, the men relax for a few minutes in their NASA jumpsuits. They have a special visitor waiting. President Nixon has stopped by to praise the astronauts for a job well done. He gave a speech, peeking at the men from outside the trailer.

The president speaks of the many people he had received goodwill messages from. He invites the astronauts to dinner at the White House and to a State dinner in Los Angeles. He also tells them he had spoken with their wives. He called the women, "... three of the greatest ladies and most courageous ladies in the whole world today ..."

The president closes by saying that because of their bravery, the week would go down as the greatest week in history. The president then asks the ship's chaplain to offer a prayer of thanksgiving. Chaplain Pierto says that the past week has been both a time of anxiety and hope. "As we try to understand and analyze the scope of this achievement for human life, our reason is overwhelmed with abounding gratitude and joy, even as we realize the increasing challenges of the future," he says. He adds that the success of the lunar landing proves just how much man could achieve. Success was possible, even when some remained unconvinced.

President Nixon welcoming the Apollo 11 crew back from their mission.

That night, the astronauts slept peacefully for nine hours.

After returning from the trip of their lifetime, the voyagers probably wanted nothing more than to see their family. Skin-to-skin reunions would have to wait. At the Ellington Air Force Base in Houston, the wives were able to speak to their husbands through a window for a short time. But for three weeks, the crew would be quarantined to make sure they hadn't brought any undesirable contaminants back to Earth.

Also in insolation would be Dr. Carpentier and engineer John Hirasaki. The quarantine trailer had arrived at Pearl Harbor (a U.S. Naval base near Honolulu, Hawaii) two days after the astronauts returned.

Next their trailer is loaded onto to a flatbed truck and driven to Hickam Field. The trailer is then flown to Houston. After arriving in Houston, the returning heroes (still trailer-confined) are paraded through the streets of Houston. Mayor Louie Welch greets the trio during a welcome home ceremony. The trailer finally arrives at its destination — the Lunar Receiving Laboratory at the Manned Spacecraft Center.

To find out if any dangerous life form had hitched a ride on the spacecraft (or the astronauts), doctors turn to mice for an answer. They expose the mice to the astronauts and the Moon rocks.

How do the astronauts occupy their time in the isolation quarters? They prepare for the inevitable debriefing and write reports; they play games and exercise; they watched TV and slog through a mound of mail, telegrams, and newspaper clips. Sometimes they simply walk to the window and gaze out hoping someone would pass by so they can wave to them!

On August 10, 1969, the *Apollo 11* astronauts were released from quarantine. All the men wanted to do was go home and relax with their families. The press had agreed to leave them alone for six weeks. Most lived up to the arrangement, but a few didn't stick to the pact. The crew reported having to make detours to avoid nagging reporters and photographers.

The public was hungry for a glimpse of the heroes. On September 13, the "Giant Step" tour began. The astronauts, their families, and a horde of

NASA officials began the tour in New York City. Four million onlookers crowded Wall Street to honor the heroes with a ticker-tape (shredded paper) parade.

Aldrin said they were told not to shake hands because someone might pull them from the convertible. From New York, the entourage flew to Chicago for another confetti-laden parade. That same night, they jetted to Los Angeles for a state dinner hosted by President Nixon. Over 1,440 people were present including politicians and celebrities. Each astronaut received a Presidential Medal of Freedom.

FAST FACT

The Presidential Medal of Freedom is the highest honor bestowed on a U.S. citizen. The award recognizes individuals who have made important contributions to the security or national interests of the United States, to world peace, to culture, or for other remarkable public or private accomplishments.

The crew made the TV rounds appearing on programs like *Meet the Press* and *Face the Nation*. They then headed back to Houston for another parade and a barbeque held at the Astrodome. Finally, they had some time alone with their families.

The second leg of the tour involved visiting 23 countries in 38 days. The tour began September 9, 1969 and ended November 5. Here are a few of the people they visited:

- England's Queen Elizabeth

- Pope Paul VI

- Japan's Emperor Hirohito

- Baudouin I and Fabiola, The King and Queen of Belgium

- Zaire President Mobutu Sese Seko.

APOLLO 11 CONSPIRACY THEORIES

Was there an actual *Apollo 11* lunar landing? If you believe conspiracy theorists the answer is no. They believe the landing was staged. Some people even claim that all of the Apollo landings were elaborate hoaxes. But why would NASA fake the landings? Some theorists accuse NASA of faking the landing to make sure the United Space won the space race. Others say NASA was greedy and wanted to keep money flowing into the agency.

The origin of the hoax theory traces back to writer Bill Kaysing. *We Never Went to the Moon* is the title of Kaysing's book, published in 1976. And fakery does not come cheap. Kaysing claims the NASA plopped down $25 billion for the six lunar missions from 1969-1972 — we'll discuss post-*Apollo 11* missions in the next chapter.

From 1956 until 1963, Kaysing was head of technical publications for the Rocketdyne (now Aerojet Rocketdyne) Research Department in California. The company was the engine contractor for the Apollo spacecraft.

According to Kaysing: "In the late '50s, when I was at Rocketdyne, they did a feasibility study on astronauts landing on the moon. They found that the chance of success was something like .0017 percent. In other words, it was hopeless." [61]

Kaysing further claims that after the rockets lifted off, the spacecraft veered to the south polar sea. The crew (in the CM) jettisoned and the spacecraft crashed. After the "mission," the crew, along with the CM, hopped aboard

---

61. Wired, 2017.

a military plane. They were dropped into the Pacific Ocean after "splashdown."

But what about the Moon rocks? The samples are also fake, according to Kaysing who says that they were created in a NASA geology lab. Was everyone in on the hoax, you ask? Kaysing claims the circle of knowledge was small. The inner circle was kept quiet with bonuses, promotions, and disguised threats.

Other well-known conspiracy theorists include Bill Brian. He published a book, *Moongate* (1982) about the alleged hoax. Brian claims that there's a cover up, but he has a different idea than Kaysing. According to Brian, "... it's possible we reached the moon with the aid of a secret zero gravity device that NASA probably reverse-engineered by copying parts of a captured extraterrestrial spaceship." [62]

Brian holds a Bachelor of Science and a Masters of Science in nuclear engineering. He says the Moon's gravity is very similar to Earth's. He thinks the Moon's atmosphere is therefore very similar to our own. In his book, he presents complex calculations that he claims prove his theories. But you don't have to be a nuclear engineer to disbelieve the landing. He adds: "The NASA transcripts of the communication between the astronauts and mission control read as if they're carefully scripted. The accounts all have a very strange flavor to them, as if the astronauts weren't really there." [63]

Some of the fuel driving the conspiracy is based on the post-*Apollo 11* press conference on August 12. To this day, people who believe the mission was a hoax point to the behavior of the astronauts during the conference. They

---

62. Wired, 2017.
63. Wired, 2017.

claim their body language, the way the spoke and looked, prove they hadn't landed on the Moon.

People threw words around describing the men as unhappy, sad, uncomfortable, and tense. Not exactly what some people expected to see on the faces of three men who had just walked into the history books. Some argue that the men were clearly hiding something (and doing so uncomfortably). Maybe they went to the moon, but they *saw something*. That's another theory. This notion asserts the astronauts reported the *something* they saw and NASA threatened them to keep it a secret. We know that's preposterous since the transcripts show the astronauts reported the flashing lights. The agency didn't appear to cover up whatever it was the astronauts saw.

In their defense, others point out the crew had just survived the journey of a lifetime. They were no doubt exhausted. They had spent many hours being interrogated by NASA officials, the press, and others. They were gearing up for their world tour, as well. A little R & R wasn't on their schedule anytime soon.

Remember, Armstrong didn't like being in the spotlight, so it's understandable he might seem tense. The astronauts had a job to do and they did it. They never really considered themselves heroes — that is a label that was slapped on them. They all were a little uncomfortable at the time speaking about their experience.

Unfortunately, without any conclusive evidence, many people still believe the landing(s) was faked.

THE ASTRONAUTS POST-APOLLO

What became of the astronauts after their historic mission? Did they return to the moon or hang up their flying gear? This section highlights what happened to each astronaut post-*Apollo 11.*

Neil Armstrong

After the lunar mission, Armstrong decided he didn't want to venture into space again. He remained with NASA until 1971 in a different position. Armstrong was Deputy Associate Administrator for Aeronautics. Then he left NASA and joined the academic community. Armstrong was a professor of aerospace engineering at the University of Cincinnati for eight years, but resigned his position at the university suddenly and without explanation.

He then became a dairy farmer, but remained active in the space community. Armstrong served as chairman of Computing Technologies for Aviation, Inc., from 1982 to 1992.

He also continued to guard his privacy. The world's most famous astronaut steered clear of the limelight. He didn't give many interviews. In 1994, Armstrong stopped signing autographs after he discovered they were being sold for huge amounts of money.

Armstrong received many awards and accolades post-Apollo, including:

- Recipient of a *Congressional Space Medal of Honor* (1978)

- Induction into the Astronaut Hall of Fame (March 19, 1993)

- Recipient of the *Congressional Gold Medal for Distinguished Astronauts* (November 16, 2011)

Armstrong's first marriage to Janet ended in divorce in 1994. He married Carol Held Knight that same year. Armstrong died August 25, 2012 at the age of 82, following complications after heart surgery.

Armstrong's legacy includes:

- A museum named in his honor: The Armstrong Air and Space Museum (**https://www.armstrongmuseum.org/about-museum**) in Wapakoneta.

- The Neil Armstrong Hall of Engineering at Armstrong's alma mater, Purdue University

- Dozens of elementary, middle, and high schools named after Neil Armstrong

- Numerous streets, buildings, and other structures bear his name

- In 2014, NASA renamed the Dryden Flight Research Center in southern California the "NASA Neil A. Armstrong Flight Research Center"

- In July 2014, NASA renamed the historic Spaceport Building at the Kennedy Space Center the Neil Armstrong Operations and Checkout Building.

- The airport where he took his first flying lessons bears his name.

After Armstrong died, his family released the following statement:

"For those who may ask what they can do to honor Neil, we have a simple request. Honor his example of service, accomplishment, and modesty, and the next time you walk outside on a clear night and see the moon smiling down at you, think of Neil Armstrong and give him a wink." [64]

President Obama said: "Neil was among the greatest of American heroes - not just of his time, but of all time." [65]

His *Apollo 11* comrades also issued public statement.

"He was the best, and I will miss him terribly," said *Apollo 11* command module pilot Michael Collins. [66]

Buzz Aldrin said: "My friend Neil took the small step but giant leap that changed the world and will forever be remembered as a landmark moment in human history. I had truly hoped that in 2019, we would be standing together along with our colleague Mike Collins to commemorate the 50th anniversary of our moon landing. Regrettably, this is not to be. Neil will most certainly be there with us in spirit." [67]

Buzz Aldrin

In the years following the *Apollo 11* mission Aldrin struggled with depression and alcoholism. He left NASA and returned to the Air Force, working as an administrator in California. Aldrin was the commandant of the Aerospace Research Pilots School at Edwards Air Force Base (1971-1972). He retired from active military duty in 1972 after 21 years of service.

Aldrin wasn't idle after leaving NASA. He studied advancements in space technology. Aldrin developed the *Aldrin Mars Cycler* — a spacecraft system

64. NASA, 2012.
65. NASA, 2012.
66. Space.com, 2012.
67. NASA, 2012.

developed for possible missions to Mars. He has also received three patents for a modular space station, a reusable rocket, and multi-crew modules.

Aldrin is still a busy man. His nonprofit, ShareSpace Foundation, focuses on STEAM (Science, Technology, Engineering, Arts, and Math) education. The group's mission is to inspire students in grades K-8 to get excited about space.

In 2007, Aldrin spoke at the grand opening of the Skywalk in the Grand Canyon. The Skywalk is a glass-bottomed observation deck, extending 70 feet from the Grand Canyon's Wall.

Another project he is involved in is the Buzz Aldrin Space Institute at Florida Tech. The institute was created in August 2015 to promote and develop Aldrin's vision of a permanent human settlement on Mars.

Aldrin has written several books, including:

Memoir/autobiography

- *Return to Earth* (1973)

- *Magnificent Desolation: The Long Journey Home from the Moon* (2009)

- *No Dream Is Too High: Life Lessons From a Man Who Walked on the Moon* (2016)

Children's Books

- *Reaching for the Moon* (2005)

- *Look to the Stars* (2009)

- *Welcome to Mars: Making a Home on the Red Planet* (2015);

Science Fiction

- *The Return* (2000)

- *Encounter with Tiber* (1996),

- *Men from Earth* (1989)

Non-fiction

Mission to Mars: My Vision for Space Exploration (2013)

Unlike the camera-shy Armstrong, Aldrin has spent a good deal of his life in the public eye. He continues to lecture and make appearances. He even showed a few dance moves in 2010 on *Dancing with the Stars*. Other places he's popped up include:

- Television appearances: *The Simpsons, 30 Rock, Numb3rs,* and *The Big Bang Theory*

- Movies: *Transformers: Dark of the Moon (2011)*

- The Disney Toy Story movie character Buzz Lightyear is modeled after Aldrin

- The MTV Music Video Award Statute (Moonman aka Buzzy) is named after Aldrin

- He collaborated with Snoop Dogg and Talib Kweli to create "Rocket Experience", a kids' song promoting space exploration (you haven't lived until you hear Aldrin rapping!)

Aldrin and his first wife Joan divorced in 1972. He married Beverly Zile in 1975. That marriage also ended in divorce. In 1988, he married Lois Driggs Cannon. Unfortunately, that marriage also ended in divorce in 2012.

Aldrin received the Congressional Gold Medal for Distinguished Astronauts (November 11, 2011) and was inducted into the Astronauts Hall of Fame (March 19, 1993).

On December 1, 2016, Aldrin was evacuated from the South Pole while part of a tourist group. He was flown to a hospital in New Zealand. Aldrin released a statement on December 3 saying he experienced shortness of breath during the trip. He also had lung congestion and altitude sickness.

Michael Collins

Like Armstrong, Collins decided Apollo 11 would be his last mission. He left NASA in January 1970. Collins was the assistant secretary of public affairs from 1970-1971 at the U.S. Department of State. He took a position as the first director of the Smithsonian Institution's National Air and Space Museum in Washington D.C. (1971-1978). Collins returned to college, completing Harvard Business School's Advanced Management Program (1974). In 1978, he became the undersecretary at the museum until 1980.

He left the museum to work at LTV Aerospace & Defense Company, where he served as Vice President from 1980-1985. He then founded Michael Collins Associates. His Washington, D.C. based firm consulted with the aerospace industry. In 1985, he was also inducted into the Astronaut Hall of Fame.

Collins is the author of four books: *Carrying the Fire* (1974); *Flying to the Moon and other Strange Places* (1976); *Liftoff: The Story of America's Adventure in Space* (1988); and *Flying to the Moon: An Astronaut's Story* (1994).

—— *FAST FACT* ——

In the 2009 television movie, *Moon Shot*, Collins was portrayed by *Walking Dead* star Andrew Lincoln.

For the *Apollo 11* 40th Anniversary, Collins provided NASA with a written statement of frequently asked questions and his answers, instead of a live media interview. Was he a recluse — someone who likes living alone or outside society? He said he wouldn't use that particular word, but he never liked the spotlight.

How did he spend his time? Collins enjoyed was painting. In fact, Collins is a gifted watercolor artist. He rarely paints space scenes though, preferring Earth's nature subjects. At the time, he also enjoyed watching football (the Washington Redskins) and a good bottle of wine (as long as it was under $10). He also didn't watch much TV with the exception of nature programs (and football).

Finally, people often want to know if Collins felt he received the amount of recognition he deserved for his role in the Apollo mission. "Lordy yes," he responded. "Oodles and oodles." [68]

The third astronaut was married to his first wife Patricia until her death in April 2014.

—— *FAST FACT* ——

All three astronauts have lunar craters and asteroids named in their honor.

68. Collins, 2009.

Chapter 9

POST-APOLLO MISSIONS

THE *APOLLO 11* LUNAR LANDING WAS THE FULFILLMENT OF President Kennedy's challenge. But it was just the beginning for NASA. Six more manned missions to the Moon followed. Let's take a look at each mission.

The patch from the Apollo program.

APOLLO 12

After the success of *Apollo 11,* NASA was ready for a second lunar landing. On November 14, 1969, *Apollo 12* launched with Charles Conrad as commander. Richard Gordon took the command module pilot's seat. The lunar module pilot was Alan Bean.

The trio landed on the Moon, November 19 and returned to Earth November 24. As in the previous mission, the CM pilot remained in orbit while the commander and LM pilot performed EVAs on the lunar surface. Conrad and Bean also examined the *Survey 3* spacecraft, which landed on the Moon two and a half years earlier. They retrieved pieces of the spacecraft for scientific examination. Among the items recovered was the spacecraft's camera. As of this writing, it is on display at the Air and Space Museum.

The mission got off to a bumpy start. It was cloudy and raining during launch. 36 seconds after liftoff, lightning struck the spacecraft. Then, 52 seconds after launch, the vehicle was struck again. These strikes caused the power to temporarily shut down. During the outage, power automatically switched to the backup battery. The crew was able to restore the main electrical power system. With no further issues, *Apollo 12* recovered and began parking orbit as planned.

The lunar crew performed two EVAs on November 19 and 20. They spent 31 hours, 31 minutes on the lunar surface.

APOLLO 13

James Lovell (commander), John Swigert (CM pilot), and Fred Haise (LM pilot) were the third group of astronauts launched to the Moon. The crew left Earth April 11, 1970 and returned April 17. The lunar landing was canceled because of a system failure.

Initially the mission was progressing smoothly. The emergency occurred on April 14 after a television broadcast from the spacecraft. One of the oxygen tanks in the service module exploded, resulting in damage to other systems. The mission was aborted to ensure the safety of the crew.

The command module Odyssey was judged unusable. The crew had to transfer to the lunar module Aquarius for the return trip. Remember, only the CM was designed to return to Earth, so there was no telling what could happen if they tried to do so in the LM. As you can imagine, it was a tense situation.

The damage to the SM was severe. "There's one whole side of that spacecraft missing," Lovell said after they jettisoned the damaged craft from the CM. The astronauts towed the SM back to Earth to protect the CM's heat shield.

The first hint that something was wrong came from Swigert as he said one of the other most famous phrases from a NASA mission:

Swigert: "Hey, we've got a problem here." [69]

CapCom: "This is Houston; say again, please."

Swigert: "Houston, we've had a problem. We've had a Main B bus undervolt."

---

69. NASA, 2016. NOTE: Unless otherwise noted, quotes/transcript info for Apollo 13 from this source.

Undervolt meant there was a drop in power in one of the CSM main electrical circuits.

> **Haise:** "And we had a pretty large bang associated with the caution and warning here."

The crew and the flight controllers knew they were in trouble. But they didn't panic. They calmly begin emergency procedures to get the astronauts home safely.

Apollo 13 was 207,000 miles from earth. The mission was 57 hours, 11 minutes since launch. The spacecraft was three days from home and had about 15 minutes of electricity left in the CM.

Houston told the guys to transfer to the LM and start powering it up, while powering down the CM.

Rather than fire the main engine of the CSM (possibly risking further damage), MCC devised a safer way to return the men home. The astronauts would coast around the Moon and use the gravitational pull to automatically send them toward Earth.

On the ground, mission control worked out the details for the splashdown and recovery. As word of the emergency spread, the nation watched, listened, prayed, and waited for the safe return of the three brave men.

Back onboard the spacecraft the astronauts had concerns. The LM is designed for two astronauts. Not only in terms of available space but consumables (oxygen, water, and batteries). In the original plan, the LM would sustain two astronauts for 60 hours. Because of the emergency, there were three men and the resources had to stretch for about 90 hours. Was it possible?

After much thought and planning, the outcome wasn't as bleak as the initial assessment. They could bring drinking water from the CM. They had about 95 hours of oxygen. If they used the power for only essential equipment, cooling water would last 23 hours after re-entry. They had 60 hours of battery life, enough to recharge the CM batteries before separation.

As the crew raced closer to Earth, it was soon time to separate from the LM. "She was a great ship," the crew agreed. [70] But now their lifeboat was no longer needed. Aquarius would burn up in the Earth's atmosphere once she was released.

The USS *Iwo Jima* was waiting to recover the voyagers. It was anchored 600 miles southeast of Samoa.

The world waited for visual confirmation. Soon a scorched Odyssey broke through the clouds.

The astronauts splashed down four miles from the recovery ship. It was 142 hours, 52 minutes, 41 seconds since they left Earth.

Only after the men were safely recovered did MCC staff take a collective breath of relief.

President Nixon awarded the astronauts the Medal of Freedom. He noted: "The three astronauts did not reach the Moon, but they reached the hearts of millions of people in America and in the world."

---

70. NASA, 2016.

--------- *FAST FACT* --

Nixon also awarded the Medal of Freedom to Sigurd A. Sjoberg, Director of Flight Operations, and to Flight Directors Glynn Lunney, Eugene Kranz, Gerald Griffin, and Milton L. Windler. Kranz is often credited as being the "cool head" at MCC during the emergency.

A statement released from the review board accurately read: "The *Apollo 13* accident, which aborted man's third mission to explore the surface of the Moon, is a harsh reminder of the immense difficulty of this undertaking." [71]

APOLLO 14

The next group of astronauts completed their lunar landing. Onboard the spacecraft:

Commander Alan B. Shepard, LM pilot Edgar D. Mitchell, and CM pilot Stuart A. Roosa. The launch date was January 31, 1971. The lunar landing took place on February 5.

By now the process was almost routine. After landing on the Moon, the crew collected samples, took photos, and performed EVAs. The lunar team completed two moonwalks. They spent a total of 9 hours, 23 minutes on the Moon's surface. At the end of the second walk, Shepard hit two golf balls into space. The CM pilot continued to orbit while the lunar module team performed their tasks. Other than a 40-minute delay at launch because of rain and clouds, the mission didn't experience any problems.

The crew splashed down on Earth February 9.

---

71. Cortright, 1970.

APOLLO 15

On July 26, 1971, NASA sent another group of astronauts to the Moon. David Scott was commander. In the pilot seats were Alfred Worden (CM) and James Irwin (LM). The LM crew successfully landed on the Moon July 30.

Scott and Irwin completed moonwalk EVAs. The total time spent on the Moon's surface was 18 hours, 35 minutes. The Lunar Roving Vehicle (LRV) was used for the first time during this mission. This allowed the crew to explore areas of the Moon further away from the landing site — about 3.10 miles (5 km). The three-man team returned to Earth August 7.

APOLLO 16

The next Apollo mission launched April 16, 1972. John Young was the spaceship's commander. Thomas Mattingly II served as CM pilot. The LM pilot was Charles Duke. The original launch date was March 17 but the mission was rescheduled because of a hardware malfunction.

The LM team performed three moonwalks, totaling 20 hours, 14 minutes. The LRV was also used, allowing the men to explore 16.78 miles (27 km) from the landing. They spent a total of 71 hours, 2 minutes on the lunar surface.

APOLLO 17

When Eugene Cernan (commander), Ronald Evans (CM pilot), and Harrison Schmitt (LM pilot) strapped into the *Apollo 17* spacecraft, they had no idea they would be the last astronauts of the Apollo program. The program ended after this sixth mission to the Moon.

Launching on December 7, 1972, the lunar landing took place December 11. The launch was postposed for 2 hours, 40 minutes because of an issue with one of the launch sequencers.

During the mission, Cernan and Schmitt performed three moonwalk EVAs. Schmitt was the first scientist to go to the Moon. The two spent 22 hours, 4 minutes performing EVAs. Using the Lunar Roving Vehicle, they ventured 18.64 miles (27 km) from home base. Total time spent on the lunar surface was 75 hours. The men returned to Earth on December 19.

APOLLO ROVING VEHICLE

The last three missions to the Moon used the Lunar Roving Vehicle to allow the astronauts to venture further from the LM. These electric vehicles were designed to operate in the Moon's low-gravity atmosphere.

The LRV's frame was 10.17 feet (3.1 meters) long. The wheelbase was 7.55 feet (2.3 meters) wide. The vehicle was hinged in the center and designed to fold for storage on the LM. The buggy was a two-seater, with an armrest in the center. A dish antenna was mounted on the front of the vehicle.

These little vehicles weren't cheap. Four vehicles built by Boeing cost $38 million. The fourth unused vehicle was used for spare parts after the Apollo missions were cancelled. Although it took only 17 months to design and build the rovers, they performed exceptionally well. Apollo 17's Schmitt said: "... the Lunar Rover proved to be the reliable, safe, and flexible lunar exploration vehicle we expected it to be. Without it, the major scientific discoveries of Apollo 15, 16, and 17 would not have been possible; and our current understanding of lunar evolution would not have been possible." [72]

---

72. Williams, 2016.

THE END OF THE APOLLO ERA

There were originally three additional scheduled Apollo missions. They were canceled due to budgetary issues. Three flights were actually canceled early. *Apollo 20* was cancelled in January 1970. The flights planned for *Apollo 15* and *Apollo 19* were nixed in September 1970. The remaining missions were then renumbered 15 through 17. Even so, NASA planned to continue manned missions but with a different goal in mind.

Although money was a key player in the program ceasing, it wasn't the only one. Another reason was public interest. Frankly, citizens started losing interest in the landings because they were becoming routine in many ways.

Although the Apollo era was over, NASA still had big ideas for the future of the space program.

TECHNOLOGIES WE HAVE THANKS TO APOLLO MISSIONS

Many of the advances we have today are because of technologies developed by NASA for the Apollo missions. These advances are called "spin-offs." NASA licenses their technology to companies that then create products. Here of some of the technological discoveries we can thank NASA for:

- Memory foam mattresses

- The Dustbuster (hand-held vacuums)

- Freeze-dried food

- Advances in computer technology

- Advances in athletic footwear

- Retractable stadium roofs

- Durette, a chemically treated fabric that doesn't burn (ideal for firefighters)

- Motion detector security systems

- Solar panels

- Non-chlorine pool purification system

- Heart monitors

- Cordless power tools

- Alternative energy sources (like liquid methane)

Chapter 10

THE U.S. SPACE PROGRAM TODAY

AFTER THE *APOLLO* PROGRAM ENDED, NASA WASN'T FIN-ished with space exploration. Today, NASA is on a mission to "… reach new heights and reveal the unknown for the benefit of humankind," according to the vision statement on their website.

Today's NASA scientists are working diligently on a range of projects including advanced rocket design and ways to send humans into deep space. NASA's Orion spacecraft is projected to shoot astronauts past the Moon. NASA also anticipates sending explorers to Mars. They don't have a launch date for the first mission yet, but is aiming for the 2030s.

Before we get too far ahead of ourselves, let's take a look at NASA projects after the Apollo era officially ended.

POST-APOLLO PROJECTS

Even before the *Apollo 11* lunar landing, President Nixon was thinking about NASA's future space programs. In February 1969, a special Space Task Group met during the spring and summer to devise a plan for space exploration.

On September 15, 1969, the committee released a report to President Nixon. NASA had ambitious goals. They pushed for the development of a space station, a reusable space shuttle, a Moon base, and manned expeditions to Mars. But the president decided not to move forward with the recommendations. In a statement released in March 1970, he wrote: "… we must also recognize that many critical problems here on this planet make high priority demands on our attention and our resources." [73]

——— *FAST FACT* ———

The first mission to orbit Mars took place on November 13, 1971 (*Mariner 9*).

Fast forward to January 5, 1972. NASA Administrator James C. Fletcher announced the president had given the green light to develop a new type of reusable spacecraft which would become known as the Space Shuttle.

Before launching the space shuttle missions, NASA tested orbiters on Earth first. On February 18, 1977, *Enterprise* (named after the *Star Trek* spaceship) performed the first of a series of test flights. The results were important in deciding whether to move forward with manned missions using the new aircraft. After successful test flights, NASA was certain the spacecraft was ready for spaceflight.

——— *FAST FACT* ———

The shuttles were 184 feet long with a wingspan of 78 feet.

---

73. Barry, 2003.

The first shuttle mission was launched on April 12, 1981. John Young and Robert Crippin were the astronauts aboard the Space Shuttle *Columbia*. The mission lasted 2 days, 6 hours, and 21 minutes.

More missions followed aboard the five shuttles: *Columbia, Challenger, Discovery, Atlantis*, and *Endeavour*. Between April 1981 and July 2011, there were 135 missions. The number of missions each shuttle flew are as follows.

Columbia: **28**

Challenger: **10**

Discovery: **39**

Endeavour: **25**

Atlantis: **33**

During the program, the shuttles travelled **542,398,878** miles — that's **21,152** orbits around the Earth.

Other important Space Shuttle milestones include:

- *Challenger:* April 4-9, 1982, the first *Challenger* flight

- *Challenger:* June 18-24, 1983 with the first female astronaut, Sally Ride, on board

- *Challenger:* August 30, 1983 with the first African-American astronaut, Guion Bluford, on board

- *Columbia:* November 28, 1983 with the first non-U.S. astronaut for a U.S. mission, Ulf Merbold of Germany, on board

- *Discovery:* August 30, 1984, the first *Discovery* shuttle mission

- *Atlantis*: August 8, 1985, the first *Atlantis* flight

- *Endeavour:* May 2-16, 1992, the first flight and the first three-person spacewalk

- *Discovery:* February 3-11, 1994 with the first Russian cosmonaut, Sergei Krikalev, on board

- *Columbia*: November 19-December 7, 1996, the longest mission at 17 days, 15 hours, 53 minutes, and 18 seconds

- *Atlantis*: July 8-21, 2011, the last mission

FAST FACT

On August 7, 1996, NASA announced that scientists had evidence (but not conclusive proof) that some form of microscopic life once existed on Mars.

FAST FACT

Story Musgrave was the only astronaut to fly aboard all five shuttles.

THE SPACE SHUTTLE *CHALLENGER* AND *COLUMBIA* DISASTERS

On January 28, 1986, the world was once again reminded of the dangers of space travel.

73 seconds after leaving Kennedy Space Center, the Space Shuttle *Challenger* exploded on live television. The crew of seven included Christa McAuliffe, an educator who was selected to participate in NASA's Teacher in Space Project. The other members were Francis Scobee, Michael Smith, Judith Resnik, Ronald McNair, Ellison Onizuka, and Gregory Jarvis.

The explosion of the Challenger on January 28, 1986.

An investigation discovered the disaster was caused by "... a failure in the joint between the two lower segments of the right Solid Rocket Motor. The specific failure was the destruction of the seals that are intended to prevent hot gases from leaking through the joint during the propellant burn of the rocket motor." [74]

In an statement addressed to the nation, President Reagan said, "Today is a day for mourning and remembering." [75]

---

74. NASA
75. Reagan, 2004.

He continued: "19 years ago, almost to the day, we lost three astronauts in a terrible accident on the ground. But we've never lost an astronaut in flight; we've never had a tragedy like this."[76]

In schools across America, students had watched the liftoff live. Reagan knew the event might have traumatized many young people. He addressed the students in his speech. He realized the tragedy was hard for some to understand but "... sometimes painful things like this happen. It's all part of the process of exploration and discovery. It's all part of taking a chance and expanding man's horizons. The future doesn't belong to the faint-hearted; it belongs to the brave. The *Challenger* crew was pulling us into the future, and we'll continue to follow them." [77]

17 years later, the United States experienced another devastating space tragedy. On February 1, 2003, the Space Shuttle *Columbia* disintegrated during re-entry. All seven astronauts died. Pieces of the ship were strewn over Texas. The 17-day science mission had launched January 16, 2003. The *Columbia* astronauts were David Brown, William McCool, Michael Anderson, Kalpana Chawla, Rick Husband, Laurel Clark, and Ilan Ramon.

According to the investigative report, "... a large piece of insulating foam from *Columbia's* external tank (ET) had come off during ascent and struck the leading edge of the left wing, causing critical damage. The damage was undetected during the mission." [78]

President George W. Bush addressed a mourning nation shortly after the catastrophe. "My fellow Americans, this day has brought terrible news and great sadness to our country," he said.[79]

---

76. Reagan, 2004.
77. Reagan, 2004.
78. NASA, 2003.
79. Bush, 2003.

Bush informed the nation that Mission Control had lost contact with the shuttle at 9:00 a.m. Shortly thereafter, debris was observed falling from the sky over Texas. "The Columbia is lost; there are no survivors," he announced. [80]

The president reminded viewers that although space travel might seem routine at this point, there are inherent dangers we shouldn't overlook. "These astronauts knew the dangers, and they faced them willingly, knowing they had a high and noble purpose in life," he continued. [81]

He told the families of the fallen astronauts that the country grieved with them. But although there was tragedy in the skies, the journey to explore space would continue. "The cause in which they died will continue. Mankind is led into the darkness beyond our world by the inspiration of discovery and the longing to understand," he said. [82]

THE SPACE SHUTTLES — WHERE ARE THEY NOW?

- Space Shuttle *Atlantis*: Kennedy Space Center Visitor Complex (**https://www.kennedyspacecenter.com/**)

- Space Shuttle *Discovery*: Steven F. Udvar-Hazy Center (**https://airandspace.si.edu/udvar-hazy-center**)

- Space Shuttle *Endeavour*: California Science Center (**https://californiasciencecenter.org/**)

- *Space Shuttle Enterprise*: Intrepid Sea, Air & Space Museum (**https://www.intrepidmuseum.org/**)

---

80. Bush, 2003.
81. Bush, 2003.
82. Bush, 2003.

The youngest person to fly on the shuttle was Sultan bin Salman bin Abdul-Aziz Al Saud. He was 28 years old when he flew aboard *Discovery* in 1985. John Glenn was the oldest at 77 years old. He flew aboard *Discovery* in 1998.

THE INTERNATIONAL SPACE STATION

The International Space Station (ISS) is an out of this world research laboratory. No literally — it's out of this world in it's in outer space. The ISS was constructed during some of the Space Shuttle missions. It was actually built in space. Parts were taken into space in pieces and put together while in orbit. The ISS orbits the Earth every 90 minutes, traveling at a speed of 17,500 miles per hour. Humans have continuously lived on the ISS since November 2000.

The International Space Station.

You can see the ISS from Earth without any special equipment. It's the largest artificial satellite ever to orbit the Earth. Want to see the space station for yourself? You can find out if the satellite is in your area at any given moment by going to **www.spotthestation.nasa.gov**.

This massive colony weighs 861,804 lbs and is as big as a football field. Unlike the cramped space of the Apollo modules, the ISS has plenty of living area — about the same amount as a typical six-bedroom house. The satellite has some of the comforts of home, most important of which include two bathrooms. There's also a gym and 360-degree viewing window.

Working in a microgravity environment, astronauts conduct scientific experiments and test new technologies. The experiments fall into six categories:

1. Biology and Biotechnology

2. Earth and Space Science

3. Educational Activities

4. Human Research

5. Physical Science

6. Technology

Unlike the Apollo missions, ISS astronauts live in space for an extended period. A typical mission about the ISS lasts about six months. In March 2016, astronaut Scott Kelly and cosmonaut Mikhail Kornienko made history by becoming the first humans to continuously live in space. They spent a total of 340 days on the ISS.

These missions help NASA learn if astronauts (and maybe one day regular people!) can live in deep space.

As the name "international" implies, astronauts from other countries use the space station. On January 29, 1998, 15 countries met and signed an International Space Station agreement. The pact established a cooperative outline for designing, developing, and operating the Space Station. Along with the United States, the cooperating countries were: Russia, Japan, Canada, Belgium, Denmark, France, Germany, Italy, the Netherlands, Norway, Spain, Sweden, Switzerland, and the United Kingdom.

FAST FACT

It's never too early to start thinking about your career choices. Interested in working for NASA? Visit their career portal at **www.nasa.gov/careers** for more information, including details on internships for college students.

One of the best ways to keep up with the ever-changing advances in space research is to go straight to the source. Be sure to bookmark the following:

NASA's website: www.nasa.gov

Social Media:

Twitter — @nasa

Facebook — **www.facebook.com/NASA**

Instagram — **www.instagram.com/nasa/**

NASA TV: www.nasa.gov/multimedia/nasatv/index.html#public

NASA Live: www.nasa.gov/nasalive

Just as the Mercury, Gemini, Apollo and Space Shuttle programs came to an end, so must our journey. Thankfully, it's not the termination of space voyages. As you have read, NASA scientists are committed to exploring the far reaches of space. As long as we have bold men and women willing to risk their lives in the name of scientific space exploration, there's no telling how far we can go and what we can achieve. Will humans land on Mars and begin a new pioneering adventure in our lifetime? Only time will tell.

CONCLUSION

IT SEEMS LIKE SINCE THE BEGINNING OF TIME MAN HAS gazed up at the stars and wondered what was out there in the great beyond. I know it sounds like a cliché but it's true. As you have read in the pages of this book, there are plenty of brave voyagers willing to leave the cozy arms of Mother Earth for the dark, unknown abyss of outer space.

The astronauts of the early programs — Gemini, Mercury, and Apollo — were pioneers. When President Kennedy issued his now famous challenge, no one knew if reaching the Moon was a realistic goal. But a remarkable thing happened. Volunteers flocked to NASA to basically serve as guinea pigs and find out for themselves if it was possible.

NASA scientists had to figure a way to get the volunteers to the moon and return them safely. Neither group hesitated. They shrugged their shoulders and *believed* it could was possible. Along the way to success, there were failures, sacrifices, and tragedy. But in the end, the people of NASA learned from their mistakes and eventually achieved success together.

New technologies were developed during these early programs. We use many of these discoveries in our everyday lives.

These early programs paved the way for a new generation of space travel. The space shuttle era enjoyed many successes, as well. Today, NASA continues to press the boundaries of possibility in space. We have humans living and working on the International Space Station. The 21st century has only furthered our understanding of space exploration as, with the internet, we now have a front-row seat and can observe what's happening in space. We can witness some events in real-time or watch recorded events at our leisure.

Maybe one day a trip to another planet will be as common as a trip to your favorite vacation spot. If so, the accolades will go to the brave men and women who were willing to risk their lives exploring the unknown, and those who will go on to do so in the future.

AUTHOR'S NOTE

MOST OF US REMEMBER WHERE WE WERE FOR IMPORTANT or tragic events. At five years old, I was too young to remember the *Apollo 11* landing. But I vividly recall the tragic events of January 1986. Like millions of people, I saw the Space Shuttle *Challenger* explosion as it happened. I was a young, wide-eyed, spunky student at the University of New Orleans. Like other students, faculty and staff, I was huddled around a TV screen when the disaster happened. I recall the look of shock on fellow students' faces. And then many of us began to cry. I shed tears for people I had never met. I cried for their families and I cried for our country.

I'm afraid to fly. I can literally count on one hand the times I've been airborne — four times. The first was a round-trip from New Orleans to Houston, Texas in the early 80s. It took 30 years before I boarded a plane again, this time a a round trip excursion from New Orleans to Washington, D.C.

Since I'm sharing, let me add this little nugget: I hate heights. Because of these two phobias, the chances I would have even considered becoming an astronaut is *zilch, nada, zero*. However, when given the chance to write this book, I was excited. I wanted to learn more about these brave men and women. I learned quite a lot and enjoyed the journey. I hope you have also enjoyed reading this book as much as I enjoyed writing it.

Pouring over hundreds of pages of mission transcripts and other documents was mesmerizing. I learned so much about our three featured astronauts. I know their distinct personalities and little quirks. I also enjoyed watching documentary footage of the missions. Have you ever watched a movie or TV program more than once? You know the outcome but you're still excited the second (or third) time around. That's how I felt while watching the liftoff and lunar landing. I knew the outcome, but I was still on the edge of my seat.

I dedicate this book to the courageous men and women who lost their lives in pursuit of space exploration. I also applaud those who went to space and returned safely. And to the three *Apollo 11* pioneers Neil Armstrong, Michael Collins, and Buzz Aldrin, a big thank you for leading the way.

AUTHOR BIO

MYRA FAYE TURNER IS A WRITER, POET, AVID COFFEE DRINKER, and children's book author. She lives in New Orleans, Louisiana with her teenaged son, Tyler. Although she doesn't fly, she's more than happy to give you a ride to the airport.

GLOSSARY

anomaly: *something that is different, strange, or out of the ordinary*

ballistic: *projectiles in motion or flight*

centrifuge: *a machine used for seperating substances*

claustrophobia: *a fear of small spaces*

commandant: *the leader or person in charge*

cryogenic: *relating to very low temperature*

declassified : *remove restrictions from*

deploy: *to use*

disengaged: *detached or unlocked from*

docking: *the process of joining together*

earmarked: *money set aside for a specific project or program*

errant: *misbehaving*

fiscal year: *an accounting period of 12 consecutive months (June 1 – July 31, for example) as opposed to a calendar year (January 1 – December 31)*

galumph: *to walk clumsily*

nonchalant: *a casual or unworried manner*

orchestrate: *to arrange or plan out in order to achieve a desired result*

precursor: *to precede or come before*

predecessor: *someone who has occupied a position previously*

telemetry: *a device for transmiting data*

trajectory: *a set path*

unison: *at the same time*

Important NASA Terms and Abbreviations

Command and Service Module (CSM): *the combined command and service module*

Command Module (CM): *the portion of the spacecraft in which the crew lived and worked*

Public Affairs Officer (PAO): *the person responsible for keeping the public informed of mission status*

Service Module (SM): *the portion of the spacecraft that housed the rockets, fuel supply, and other mission essentials*

Spacecraft Communicator (CapCom): *the designated person (always an astronaut) responsible for communicating with the crew during missions*

Launch Control Center (LCC): *responsible for launching all manned space flights; located at the Kennedy Space Center in Florida*

Mission Control Center (MCC): *responsible for handling all manned missions from launch to return to Earth; located at the Johnson Space Center in Houston*

Flight Director (FD): *the person in charge of the overall operation of the mission*

BIBLIOGRAPHY

Thimmesh, Catherine. *Team Moon*. New York: Houghton Mifflin, 2006. Print.

Nelson, Craig. *Rocket Men: The Epic Story of the First Men on the Moon.* New York: Viking, 2009. Print.

Graham, Ian. *Space Travel.* New York: DK Pub., 2004. 16, 25-26, 28, 29. Print.

Chaikin, Andrew, and Victoria Kohl. *Mission Control, This Is Apollo: The Story of the First Voyages to the Moon.* New York: Penguin Group, 2009. 7, 8,9. Print.

Barbree, Jay. Neil Armstrong: A Life of Flight. New York: St. Martin's, 2014. Print.

Woods, David, Ken MacTaggert, and Frank O'Brien. "Apollo Fight Journal." *NASA.* NASA, 10 Feb. 2017. Web. 14 Oct. 2017.

"Apollo 11 Lunar Surface Journal." *NASA.* NASA, 17 Dec. 2015. Web. 19 Oct. 2017.

Introduction

"The Decision to Go to the Moon: President John F. Kennedy's May 25, 1961 Speech before a Joint Session of Congress." *National Aeronautics and Space Administration NASA History Office*. National Aeronautics and Space Administration, 29 Oct. 2013. Web. 13 Sept. 2017.

Bibliography.com Editors. "Alan Shepard." *Biography.com*. A&E Networks Television, 11 Dec. 2014. Web. 14 Sept. 2017.

History.com Staff. "This Day in History: Sputnik Launched." *History.com*. A&E Television Networks, 2009. Web. 14 Sept. 2017.

Elizabeth Howell. "Sputnik: The Space Race's Opening Shot." *Space.com*. Purch, 27 Nov. 2012. Web. 14 Sept. 2017.

Pruitt, Sarah. "What Really Happened to Yuri Gagarin, the First Man in Space?" *History.com*. A&E Television Networks, 12 Apr. 2016. Web. 14 Sept. 2017.

National Aeronautics and Space Act of 1958, As Amended. Washington, D.C.: National Aeronautics and Space Administration, 2005. 4. Print.

Manchester, William. "John F. Kennedy." *Encyclopædia Britannica*. Encyclopædia Britannica, Inc., 22 June 2017. Web. 18 Sept. 2017.

Freidel, Frank, and Hugh Sidey. "John F. Kennedy." *The White House*. The United States Government, 16 Aug. 2017. Web. 18 Sept. 2017.

Dewdney, John C., Richard E. Pipes, Martin McCauley, and Robert Conquest. "Union of Soviet Socialist Republics. *Encyclopædia Britannica*. Encyclopædia Britannica, Inc., 10 Mar. 2017. Web. 19 Sept. 2017.

Harwood, William. "JFK's Legacy: Setting America on Course for the Moon." *CBS News*. CBS Interactive, 21 Nov. 2003. Web. 19 Sept. 2017.

Chapter 1

Tyson, Neil DeGrasse. *Space Chronicles: Facing the Ultimate Frontier*. New York: W.W. Norton, 2012. Print.

History.com Staff. "Cold War History." *History.com*. A&E Television Networks, 2009. Web. 21 Sept. 2017.

Elizabeth Dohrer. "Laika the Dog & the First Animals in Space." *Space.com*. Purch, 30 May 2017. Web. 21 Sept. 2017.

Staff, Space News and SPACE.com. "Timeline: 50 Years of Spaceflight." *Space.com*. Purch, 28 Sept. 2012. Web. 21 Sept. 2017.

Smith, Woody. "Explorer Series of Spacecraft." *NASA*. NASA, 22 Feb. 2006. Web. 21 Sept. 2017.

"Pioneer 1." *National Aeronautics and Space Administration*. NASA. Web. 23 Sept. 2017.

The Editors of Encyclopædia Britannica. "Luna." *Encyclopædia Britannica*.

Encyclopædia Britannica, Inc., 20 Aug. 2013. Web. 23 Sept. 2017.

"Discoverer 1." *National Aeronautics and Space Administration*. NASA. Web. 23 Sept. 2017.

"Pioneer 4." NASA Jet Propulsion Lab. NASA. Web. 23 Sept. 2017.

"Able and Baker." *Smithsonian National Air and Space Museum*. Smithsonian Institution, 22 Mar. 2017. Web. 23 Sept. 2017.

"Discoverer 4." *National Aeronautics and Space Administration*. NASA. Web. 23 Sept. 2017.

"Luna 3." *National Aeronautics and Space Administration*. NASA. Web. 23 Sept. 2017.

"The Television Infrared Observation Satellite Program (TIROS)." *NASA Science*. NASA, 22 May 2016. Web. 24 Sept. 2017.

"Discoverer 13." *National Aeronautics and Space Administration*. NASA. Web. 25 Sept. 2017.

NASA Content Administrator. "Project Echo." *NASA*. NASA, 4 Aug. 2017. Web. 25 Sept. 2017. <https://www.nasa.gov/centers/langley/about/project-echo.html>.

"Discoverer 14." *National Aeronautics and Space Administration*. NASA. Web. 25 Sept. 2017.

Williams, Dr. David. "The Apollo 1 Tragedy." *NASA*. NASA, 4 Mar. 2011. Web. 25 Sept. 2017.

Pyle, Rod. *Destination Moon: The Apollo Missions in the Astronauts' Own Words*. New York: Harper Collins, 2005. 13,18. Print.

"Apollo 7." *National Aeronautics and Space Administration*. NASA. Web. 25 Sept. 2017.

"Apollo 8." *National Aeronautics and Space Administration*. NASA. Web. 25 Sept. 2017.

"Apollo 9." *National Aeronautics and Space Administration*. NASA. Web. 25 Sept. 2017.

"Apollo 10." *National Aeronautics and Space Administration*. NASA. Web. 25 Sept. 2017.

Purcell, Michael. "Combined Military Operations: The Practical Challenges of US-Russia Cooperation in Syria (Part II)." *Center on Global Interests*. Center on Global Interests, 15 Sept. 2016. Web. 03 Oct. 2017.

Robinson, Peter. "Tear Down This Wall." *National Archives and Records Administration*. National Archives and Records Administration, Summer 2007. Web. 03 Oct. 2017.

Biography.com Editors. "John Glenn". *Biography.com*. A&E Networks Television, 06 Apr. 2017. Web. 04 Oct. 2017.

Chapter 2

Whiting, Melanie. "NASA Astronauts Homepage." *NASA*. NASA, 04 Jan. 2016. Web. 26 Sept. 2017.

Link Mae Mills. "Space Medicine in Project Mercury." *National Aeronautics and Space Administration*. NASA. Web. 04 Oct. 2017.

"Deke Slayton." *National Aeronautics and Space Administration*. NASA, June 1993. Web. 2 Oct. 2017.

Hitt, David, and Rebecca Dorfmueller. "The History of Spacesuits." *National Aeronautics and Space Administration*. NASA, 16 Sept. 2008. Web. 04 Oct. 2017.

Chapter 3

Dixon-Engel, Tara, and Mike Jackson. *Neil Armstrong: One Giant Leap for Mankind*. Sterling, 2008.

Dunbar, Brian. "Biography of Neil Armstrong." *NASA*. NASA, 10 Mar. 2015. Web. 29 Sept. 2017.

Aldrin, Buzz, and Ken Abraham. *No Dream Is Too High: Life Lessons from a Man Who Walked on the Moon*. National Geographic, 2016.

Biography.com Editors. "Buzz Aldrin." *Biography.com*, A&E Networks Television, 22 Sept. 2017.

Biography.com Editors. "Michael Collins." *Biography.com*. A&E Networks Television, 09 Jan. 2017. Web. 02 Oct. 2017.

Collins, Michael. *Carrying the Fire: An Astronaut's Journeys*. New York: Farrar, Straus and Giroux, 1974. Print.

Chapter 4

"Apollo 11: About the Spacecraft." *Smithsonian National Air and Space Museum.* Smithsonian. Web. 11 Oct. 2017.

"Apollo 11 Command and Service Module (CSM)." *NASA Space Science Data Coordinated Archive.* National Aeronautics and Space Administration. Web. 11 Oct. 2017.

"Apollo 11 Lunar EASEP." *NASA Space Science Data Coordinated Archive.* National Aeronautics and Space Administration. Web. 11 Oct. 2017.

Teitel, Amy Shira. "How Did the Apollo Command and Service Modules Separate?" *Popular Science.* Bonnier, 01 Apr. 2016. Web. 10 Oct. 2017.

Harbaugh, Jennifer. "Biography of Wernher von Braun." *National Aeronautics and Space Administration.* NASA, 18 Feb. 2016. Web. 10 Oct. 2017.

Hutchinson, Lee. "Going Boldly: Behind the Scenes at NASA's Hallowed Mission Control Center." *Ars Technica.* Conde Nast, 31 Oct. 2012. Web. 10 Oct. 2017.

Bray, Nancy. "Launch Control Center Home Page." *NASA.* NASA, 07 Aug. 2013. Web. 10 Oct. 2017.

Canright, Shelly. "The People Behind the Astronauts." *NASA.* NASA, 10 Apr. 2009. Web. 11 Oct. 2017.

Eugene F. Kranz." *NASA.* NASA. Web. 12 Oct. 2017.

Jones, Eric. "Apollo 11 Crew Information." *NASA.* NASA, 7 Sept. 2012. Web. 14 Oct. 2017. <https://www.hq.nasa.gov/alsj/a11/a11.crew.html>.

Ott, Tim. "Katherine G. Johnson." *Biography.com.* A&E Networks Television, 25 Sept. 2017. Web. 15 Oct. 2017. <https://www.biography.com/people/katherine-g-johnson-101016>.

Smith, Yvette. "The Making of the Apollo 11 Mission Patch." *NASA*. NASA, 14 July 2016. Web. 20 Oct. 2017. <https://www.nasa.gov/feature/the-making-of-the-apollo-11-mission-patch>.

Chapter 8

"Apollo 11 Spacecraft Commentary." *National Aeronautics and Space Administration*. NASA. Web. 1 Oct. 2017.

Staff, Wired. "The Wrong Stuff." *Wired*. Conde Nast, 05 June 2017. Web. 2 Nov. 2017.

Pearlman, Robert. "Congress Renames NASA Flight Center After Neil Armstrong." *Space.com*. Purch, 24 Jan. 2014. Web. 9 Nov. 2017.

"Statements on the Passing of Neil Armstrong." *National Aeronautics and Space Administration*. NASA, 26 Aug. 2012. Web. 10 Nov. 2017.

Collins, Michael. "Statement From Apollo 11 Astronaut Michael Collins." *National Aeronautics and Space Administration*. NASA, 15 July 2009. Web. 3 Nov. 2017.

Pearlman, Robert. "Neil Armstrong, First Man to Walk on Moon, Dies at 82." Space.com. Purch, 25 Aug. 2012. Web. 10 Nov. 2017.

CNN Library. "Neil Armstrong Fast Facts." *CNN*. Turner Broadcasting, 1 Sept. 2017. Web. 10 Nov. 2017.

CNN Library. "Buzz Aldrin Fast Facts." *CNN*. Turner Broadcasting, 26 Apr. 2017. Web. 10 Nov. 2017.

CNN Library. "Michael Collins Fast Facts." *CNN*. Turner Broadcasting, 26 Oct. 2017. Web. 10 Nov. 2017.

Chapter 9

"Apollo 13 "Houston We've Got a Problem." *NASA Space Science Data Coordinated Archives*. NASA, 15 July 2016. Web. 3 Nov. 2017.

Cortright, Edgar. "Report of Apollo 13 Review Board" Letter to Thomas 0. Paine. 5 June 1970. *NASA.* NASA. Web. 12 Nov. 2017.

Williams, Dr. David. "The Apollo Lunar Roving Vehicle." *NASA Space Science Data Coordinated Archives.* NASA, 19 May 2016. Web. 2 Nov. 2017.

Williams, Dr. David. "The Apollo Program (1963 - 1972)." *NASA Space Science Data Coordinated Archives.* NASA, 16 Sept. 2013. Web. 3 Nov. 2017.

Williams, Dr. David. "Apollo 18 Through 20 -The Cancelled Missions." *NASA Space Science Data Coordinated Archives.* NASA, 11 Dec. 2003. Web. 3 Nov. 2017.

"Benefits from Apollo: Giant Leaps in Technology." *National Aeronautics and Space Administration.* NASA, July 2004. Web. 5 Nov. 2017.

"Neil Armstrong (1930-2012): NASA Remembers an American Icon." *Space.com.* Purch, 25 Aug. 2012. Web. 13 Nov. 2017.

Chapter 10

Barry, Bill, and Steve Garber. "A Chronology of Defining Events in NASA History, 1958-1998" *National Aeronautics and Space Administration History Division.* NASA, 3 Jan. 2003. Web. 6 Nov. 2017.

"Report of the Presidential Commission on the Space Shuttle Challenger Accident Chapter IV: The Cause of the Accident." *National Aeronautics and Space Administration.* NASA. Web. 5 Nov. 2017.

Reagan, President Ronald. "Explosion of the Space Shuttle Challenger Address to the Nation, January 28, 1986." *National Aeronautics and Space Administration.* NASA, 7 June 2004. Web. 10 Nov. 2017.

National Aeronautics and Space Administration. "Columbia Crew Survival Investigation Report." (2003): XIX. Print.

Bush, George. "President Addresses Nation on Space Shuttle Columbia Tragedy Remarks by the President on the Loss of Space Shuttle Columbia." *National Aeronautics and Space Administration.* NASA, 1 Feb. 2003. Web. 10 Nov. 2017.

"Reference Guide to the International Space Station." *National Aeronautics and Space Administration.* NASA, 5 May 2015. Web. 10 Nov. 2017.

Rainey, Kristine. "Space Station Research Experiments." *NASA.* NASA, 01 Apr. 2015. Web. 10 Nov. 2017.

Sharp, Tim. "International Space Station: Facts, History & Tracking." *Space.com.* Purch, 5 Apr. 2015. Web. 12 Nov. 2017.

"Space Shuttle." *National Aeronautics and Space Administration.* NASA, 3 Aug. 2013. Web. 10 Nov. 2017.

INDEX